The Fords

NEW JERSEY

the Fords *of*

NEW JERSEY

POWER & FAMILY
DURING AMERICA'S FOUNDING

Jude M. Pfister

Charleston — London

THE
History
PRESS

Published by The History Press
Charleston, SC 29403
www.historypress.net

Front cover images: *Courtesy of the Genealogical and Memorial History of the State of New Jersey and Harpers Ferry Center National Historical Park Art Collection.*
Back cover images: *Courtesy of Morristown National Historical Park.*

First published 2010

Manufactured in the United States

ISBN 978.1.60949.007.2

Library of Congress Cataloging-in-Publication Data

Pfister, Jude M.
The Fords of New Jersey : power and family during America's founding / Jude Pfister.
p. cm.
Includes bibliographical references and index.
ISBN 978-1-60949-007-2
1. Ford family. 2. Morristown (N.J.)--Biography. 3. Morris County (N.J.)--Biography. 4. Morristown (N.J.)--Social life and customs--18th century. 5. Morristown (N.J.)--Social life and customs--19th century. 6. Power (Social sciences)--New Jersey--Morristown--History. 7. Families--New Jersey--Morristown--History. 8. Businessmen--New Jersey--Morristown--Biography. 9. Iron industry and trade--New Jersey--Morristown--History. 10. Morristown (N.J.)--Economic conditions. I. Title.
F144.M9P44 2010
974.9'74--dc22
2010042644

To my wife, Miriam

Select members of the Ford Family of Morris County

John Ford
circa 1675–1721/2

Elizabeth (Freeman) Ford
1681–1772

Jacob Ford Sr.
1705–1777

Hannah (Baldwin) Ford
1701–1777

Jacob Ford Jr.
1738–1777

Theodosia (Johnes) Ford
1741–1824

Gabriel Ford
1765–1849

Frances (Gualdo) Ford
1767–1853

Henry A. Ford
1793–1872

Jane (Millen) Ford
1804–circa 1867

Contents

CONTENTS

PREFACE

In many ways, this book is a logical follow up to *The Jacob Ford Jr. Mansion; The Storied History of a New Jersey Home*. While both books complement each other, they are also meant to be stand-alone works. This work will concentrate on the way in which the family became important through the iron industry and their utilization of the means at their disposal to allow for their financial and political rise beginning in 1701. This will be accomplished by looking at the various aspects of the society in which the Fords lived. Greater emphasis will be given to the wider community in an effort to portray the societal motivations that impacted the family. Therefore this work is not a genealogical study, and it will offer little for anyone interested solely in that pursuit.

The story of the Ford family in Morris County, New Jersey—for the purposes of this book—covers about 175 years, from 1701 to 1873. This period represents the arrival of John Ford in the colony and the establishment of the Ford line that will ultimately lead to Henry A. Ford, whose death occurred in 1872. Henry Ford, the great-great-grandson of John Ford, initiates the sale of the last and the most visually significant portion of the Ford family legacy in Morristown: the mansion on the plot of land that had been in the family since the early eighteenth century. The mansion was a symbol of the family's success when it was built in 1772 and represented the financial possibilities available in the burgeoning colonial American economy. By 1873, it was a symbol of the past and held little appeal to the descendants as an ancestral seat.

Fully integrated and well established as a founding American family, although not of the "Mayflower family" variety, the Fords by 1870 had grown in their view of the historical past relating to the mansion. The almost worshipful type of history (bordering on a religious fervor) that came to dominant America by 1876, the year of the American centennial, seemingly did not appeal to that generation in 1873.[1] The Fords had played their role as a family with significant contributions to America's founding decades. More importantly, the mansion had played its role. It was time for the Fords and their mansion to enter history.

With so little personal information about the Fords available, much of the story will by necessity be drawn from those records that show the Fords from a business perspective, and only peripherally approach their personal lives. From this, a plausible outline of the lives they led will emerge. There are some exceptions: the later family members tend to have more surviving manuscripts pertaining to them; also, there is just enough remaining of Theodosia Ford's business activities to piece together a view of this forgotten and overlooked seminal family figure. Finally, this work seeks to examine an aspect of the Fords' life that will enable readers to look at one segment of the challenges they faced in the transition from colonist to citizen.

This work claims no comprehensiveness outside of the several specific episodes covered. There is much, much more to the Ford story than is contained herein. It is hoped that other researchers and writers with the time and energy to study the array of manuscripts left behind from a multitude of sources will be inspired by this short introduction to the Fords' lives, their work and the world in which they lived.

Acknowledgements

S pecial thanks are due to Bette Epstien of the New Jersey state archives, who graciously provided copies of the wills of several generations of Fords from the state archives collection. Special thanks to Alan Shaw of the Washington Association of New Jersey. And special thanks as well to Suzanne Hahn of the Indiana Historical Society. Christine Jochem of the Morristown Public Library graciously made her collection available, and Bonnie-Lynn Nadzeika of the Morris County Historical Society granted permission to quote widely from an exhibit catalog. Kevin Perry is also to be noted for developing the charts found in Appendix D that come from the exhibit catalog prepared by the Morris County Historical Society. Thanks are due as well to Whitney Tarella, Amber Allen and to The History Press, an enormously talented and professional staff that deserves acknowledgement.

The men and women of the Washington Association of New Jersey and the National Park Service are ultimately to be thanked for pursuing the Ford family papers when they came up for sale in the early 1970s. Their vision and aspiration for the Morristown National Historical Park (NHP) helped to move the park beyond the narrow confines of Washington hagiology. Through their foresight, they opened an entirely new approach to the study of Morristown NHP. No longer just another "Washington slept here" site, which demanded a perfunctory visit, the Ford mansion now had an individual life through its builders, the Ford family. It had a family to speak for themselves through their papers, and however limited, it allowed them to tell their story after two hundred years.

The continued dedication of the Washington Association of New Jersey, and the continued preservation work of the National Park Service, enables the past to tell its stories to new generations that may not always think about history or America's founding in the same way as Americans did a century ago. To be relevant, or even to hope to be relevant, the real people—not just the heroes and big names—need a voice. The Washington Association of New Jersey and the National Park Service are committed to giving them that voice.

Acknowledgement must be made to Randy Turner, superintendent of the Morristown NHP, who agreed to let me take time to work on this project. My curatorial colleague, Joni Rowe, provided many leads and ideas. Krystal Poelstra patiently provided research assistance and technical knowledge.

Those who have read the manuscript and offered criticism and editing have made the book more readable and more compelling as a story. They include Debbie Van Buren, Anne DeGraaf and Gordon Ward. Their insight and careful judgment have prevented many errors. What errors that may have slipped past their keen eyes are mine and mine alone.

Introduction

The Family and Community, in Brief

The story of the Ford family of Morris County New Jersey begins in colonial America through a venue that was somewhat unique to a small section of northern New Jersey. The iron business fueled the eighteenth-century development of northern New Jersey in the way that tobacco, rice or cotton provided a financial catalyst for some Southern colonies. The Fords were part of this economic expansion in New Jersey and quickly became major participants in the industrial transformation taking place. This story will focus on the Ford family and their rise to prominence through the iron industry and the subsequent story of their civic involvement over a century and a half of turbulent times as the disparate colonies transformed into a country. The family established their place in the community in Morris County from their earliest arrival in the colony. They did this not through social promotion but rather through industry, hard work and sacrifice. Through difficult legal challenges to their business interests lasting decades, they doggedly kept their focus and moved forward.

Their involvement in the business ventures available through the iron industry brought other opportunities too. Politically, New Jersey during the eighteenth century was expanding rapidly as settlers and land claims vied for prominence within the soon-to-be-outdated proprietor system of government leftover from the late seventeenth century. Although other families rose to prominence through similar channels, the Fords held a unique place among aspiring families in that they held the family fortune and influence together much longer than most—well into the nineteenth century. This is more compelling when it is understood that two of the main members of the family died within a week of each other at the beginning of 1777—not too long after the start of the Revolution—leaving a mother to deal with five children, a war and a business. In addition to the two main members in terms of the family business, two other members died over the summer of 1777: Hannah Ford, wife of Jacob Sr., and Phoebe Ford, daughter of Jacob Jr. It is no exaggeration to say that 1777 was probably one of the most difficult years for Theodosia Ford, widow of Jacob Jr. and functional head of the family after 1777.

Through the upheavals of the revolutionary period, the founding of the American republic and through the nineteenth century and Civil War (in which one of Henry Ford's sons died at the infamous Andersonville prison camp), the Fords held together amid wrenching national and personal calamities. The Fords represent more than just their own struggles. Through the lens of their activities, we can also see the development of a regional and American story. The rise of the iron industry, the establishment of a legal system, the twists and turns of economic markets and the creation of a nation all contribute to the story of the Fords and indeed allow us to see their contributions as well to the unfolding events of history.

Understanding the Fords is a process not altogether easy. Their legacy through the written word is sparse. What exists is primarily of a business nature, rather than personal. While this may have been intentional on their part, it makes the job of those who wish to understand them more difficult. Given these limitations, it will at times be necessary to fashion their story by creating an aggregate of similar scenarios to produce a plausible narrative. With this in mind, the story of the Fords (the Ford male line that runs from John, to Jacob Sr., to Jacob Jr., to Gabriel and to Henry) and the larger story of their times can be made quite compelling.

We are all familiar with stories about someone reading a diary or journal of a person from the past. The feeling of intimacy in the moments when you enter the private thoughts of someone dead for two hundred years can be quite a powerful experience. Coming face to face as it were with the past in such a real and powerful way lessens the distance between us and the past. Reading the real, unedited thoughts and feelings of someone brings us closer to understanding ourselves a little too. We are somewhat humbled when we realize that someone two hundred years ago, three hundred years ago or even further back in time had the same idea or emotional response we have had to a similar situation, and yet we thought we were quite unique and alone in our reaction. Therefore, trying to better understand the past more is a challenge very much worth taking—because it helps us understand ourselves. And with the Fords, this challenge is quite substantial given the lack of firsthand records in existence today. But the greater the challenge, the greater still the feeling of having actually met a member of the Ford family from some small glimpse that survives through their records.

John Ford's Grandson and the Mansion

The Jacob Ford Jr. family was fully American, albeit colonial, in 1772. The family by this time had ties in the colonies that stretched back over one hundred years. In 1772, ten years after his 1762 marriage, Ford Jr. would commence to build his family's mansion on a "low Piedmont hill east of the town center and just south of the Whippany river."[2] The mansion was situated on the property at the confluence of two major roads connecting the old towns of Elizabethtown and Newark. The mansion was well suited to serve the role of the visual representation of the Ford family's power and influence. The Fords' mansion, however, represented not so much an attempt at portraying the family wealth in a needlessly extravagant way. Rather, the Fords' mansion was designed to identify their status as civil leaders and prominent community participants. The mansion truly was a family home; for in the beginning when it was built, three generations were living together at once. Prior to building the mansion, four generations lived together in their Mount Hope, New Jersey home.

The Jacob Ford Jr. mansion. *Morristown National Historical Park.*

The Fords were not interested in displaying their wealth for the simple fact of display. As staunch Presbyterians, the family generally eschewed such overt displays of finery. While it is difficult to put aside a nine-thousand-square-foot home as a vision of fiscal restraint, it is more palatable when it is understood that the mansion was designed to house three generations of the family. It is no wonder then that the Fords decided to build their mansion not so much to present the family as a commercial force to be dealt with, but rather to identify themselves as leaders and co-workers in the task of creating the Morristown community.[3] The Fords were prominent members of the community in terms of church, social and civic responsibilities and had a significant level of leadership in the small town.

The Fords who built the mansion, Jacob Jr. and Theodosia, had four children who survived to adulthood (a fifth child born in the new house died before she was two). Of those who survived, Gabriel, the second eldest, became the most important in terms of the mansion and maintaining the family property later in his life.

Within quick succession in 1777, Mrs. Ford was dealt several severe blows emotionally. Her husband, Jacob Ford Jr., builder of the mansion, died of pneumonia on January 11; at the time of his death, Ford Jr. was a colonel commanding the Morris County Militia. Her father-in-law, Ford Sr., died January 19, just a week later. Several months later in June 1777, her youngest child, a girl named Phoebe, died in the mansion. Shortly after that, her mother-in-law, Hannah Ford, died. In addition to all of this, the Continental army's winter encampment of 1777 in Morristown was taking place. Compounding that event, thirty-five members of the Delaware Light Infantry Regiment, commanded by Thomas Rodney, were billeted at the mansion for two weeks in January, during which time both Jacob Fords died. No doubt this was an extremely emotional and difficult time for Mrs. Ford. Fortunately though, "the solid reputation established by her late husband and father-in-law were…[substantial] assets."[4]

Mrs. Ford, only in her late thirties, was left to raise and educate her four remaining children: Timothy, Gabriel, Elizabeth and Jacob III. By the terms of her husband's will, her father-in-law, Ford Sr., was to have received and managed the mansion and the grounds while she was provided the means for the education of the children. Unfortunately, the untimely death of Ford Sr. the same month as his son put a tremendous burden on Mrs. Ford. Upon her father-in-law's death, the property was divided among the children, with Mrs. Ford acting as guardian for their inheritance until the children reached legal age. The house continued to be jointly owned by the children until Gabriel bought out his brothers and sister in 1805.[5] Mrs. Ford had life tenancy in the mansion, dying there in 1824.[6]

MORRISTOWN

Morristown itself began as an unplanned community around the Presbyterian church, which was built in 1738–1740. The construction of the church was financially supported by Jacob Ford Sr., although he did not donate land. Ford Sr.'s funding allowed for the construction of the steeple.[7] The Presbyterian Church was a bulwark of the Morristown village community for decades. By 1772, only one other church existed, a Baptist denomination. The church was built in a section of land that had originally been part of the parcel of lands controlled by the East Jersey Council of Proprietors.[8]

The Morristown area, known as West Hanover, was part of a 5,711-acre area controlled by five members of the Proprietary Council.[9] In 1739, the year of the Presbyterian church being built, Morris County was created. The provincial legislature had accepted a petition by the leading citizens in the northern part of Hunterdon County to create the new county.[10] Among those citizens signing the petition to form the new county was Jacob Ford Sr., father of the builder of the mansion. Being approved, the new county would be named Morris after the governor of the province, Lewis Morris. Morris, who in 1738 had become the first royal governor specifically for New Jersey, also lent his name to the village of Morristown.[11]

By 1750, the village of Morristown had slightly over 100 inhabitants. On the eve of the American Revolution the village of Morristown had about 250 inhabitants. Morris County had a population of approximately 10,500 at the time of the outbreak of the Revolution in 1775.[12] This number is a ten-fold increase from when the county was established in 1739.

These demographics are very important when considering the eventual development of progress of the American Revolution. The revolutionary period was truly multifaceted. The war was fought at any given place and time on economic, social, political and legal grounds and, in some cases, just on a sense of orneriness.

Part 1

The Development of New Jersey

Without the rise of the colony and later state of New Jersey, the Ford family of Morris County would not have been a story worth telling. It is because the conditions existed from the earliest days of colonial settlement in the seventeenth century of what eventually became New Jersey to allow certain families to gain prominence. The Fords were one of many who happened to find the right mixture of determination, knowledge and luck to make their world a success. It is therefore that this work begins with a discussion of the settlement of the colony and of how that settlement was fashioned politically, economically and socially.

Chapter 1

EIGHTEENTH-CENTURY NEW JERSEY

POLITICAL BACKGROUND

By claiming the territory in 1623, the Dutch were the first to colonize New Netherland (later New Jersey), which stretched north into present-day New York and south to present-day Delaware. The most successful Dutch settlements in New Netherland were west across the Hudson River from New Amsterdam (later New York) in what is today eastern New Jersey. Hugh swaths of New Netherland were unsettled when the English, in turn, claimed the area in 1664.

John Ford, the first in the Ford family line this work will examine, arrived in New Jersey just before the two proprietary colonies, East and West Jersey, became one royal colony. This combining of the provinces occurred for the sake of greater governmental control in 1702. The extent to which John Ford was impacted by, participated in or even knew much about the governmental control system used by the proprietors is simply unknown. As a resident of New Jersey in the first decade of the eighteenth century, he would have been a witness—had he chosen—to an interesting display of power exhibited by the competing factions.

As a new arrival with more pressing concerns, John Ford perhaps viewed as unimportant the politics in a far-off place like England. Also, his position in the near Highland region of New Jersey insulated him somewhat from the activities taking place in the northeastern coastal communities where much of the agitation was occurring. Regardless of what John Ford experienced, he was able to set the stage for the expansion of his family far beyond anything of which he had been accustomed.

THE PROPRIETORS

In 1664, James, Duke of York, brother of the Stuart monarch Charles II, acquired title from his brother to a vast area of the mid-Atlantic seaboard that included New Jersey. James, in turn, transferred the New Jersey area over to his friends Sir George Carteret and John, Lord Berkeley. Berkeley sold his rights in 1674, a move not recognized by the king. Nonetheless, this sale prompted the creation of the east–west boundary between Carteret's East Jersey (the recognized area) and West Jersey, the former Berkeley lands. This recognized and unrecognized division was further complicated when Carteret died in 1680 and his land—East Jersey—was sold to numerous Quaker investors, including William Penn.

With their leaders debating over who owned what and where boundary lines should be placed, residents like John Ford were left to wonder about the validity of their individual land claims. "The failure of the Berkeley-Carteret proprietorship to recognize titles granted before the arrival of Governor Carteret was a source of prolonged irritation."[13] Settlers were constantly pitted between the proprietors and the royal officials, who saw themselves as the ultimate authority. Settlers saw no clear path for establishing a lasting pattern of government amid the chaos of competing officials. "Adjustment of conflicting land claims was the most annoying and distracting feature of New Jersey history during the colonial period."[14] Also thrown into the mix were the religious expectations of some of the later proprietors of heavenly establishments on earth that compounded the settlers' irritation and confusion.

Great emphasis was placed in the later seventeenth century on more clearly defining the east–west boundary and this helped to further land settlement, although it did not reduce confusion over land ownership. "Their [settlers] main grievance was against the proprietors who, to them, seemed guilty of gross neglect."[15] Because of this compounded confusion, both Jerseys experienced needless growing pains. "The uncertainties regarding the right of government and free trade discouraged the coming of both settlers and venture capital."[16]

The chaos over who controlled the Jerseys continued for over twenty years until the new century in 1700. "With continuing disturbances in both Jersey's, the British authorities were bombarded with reports and pleas to do something."[17] The simmering dispute between inhabitants and the proprietors was nearing a boiling point. "The line of cleavage between the two rival factions, proprietary and anti-proprietary, was naturally aggravated, because frequently a majority of the council held large proprietary estates, while in the assembly opinion favored the people who claimed lands under counter-proprietary titles."[18]

A SOLUTION

In 1701, both sides sent virtual ultimatum petitions to England asking for a settlement by someone with royal authority. Lewis Morris had been appointed an agent for the proprietors and was in England (each side would always keep a representative in London to attend to their business) arguing their case. After months of negotiations, both sets of proprietors, East and West, agreed to give up their pretense to governing the colony. Queen Anne agreed to the settlement in April 1702. The proprietors acknowledged "that they had no right to exercise the powers of government, [that] they willingly surrendered their pretenses in order that Her Majesty might appoint a governor who with the consent of the assembly and the approbation of the crown would make the laws and administer them."[19]

The proprietors continued to operate on a business level though. "The fact that the governing power of the province after 1702 had no right or title to the soil is the salient and distinctive feature of New Jersey, as distinguished from other colonies."[20] This meant that while the British crown had the right to administer the colony on a political basis, it did not own, nor could it distribute, any actual land. The "title to [the] land was held by the proprietors of East and West Jersey, whose affairs were actually administered by two councils or boards, one for each division."[21] The council for East Jersey was "an aristocratic organization of wealthy landowners."[22] Their job was to examine "the right to land titles, [purchase] land from the Indians, [rent] land to the colonists, and [transact] such other business as properly came to their attention."[23] No proprietor, except Lewis Morris who later became royal governor, held any important positions in the new royal government.

WHAT IT LOOKED LIKE

The physical landscape that confronted the settlers in the early seventeenth century was naturally much different than we experience today. "Pre-colonial vegetation was primarily oak forest, broken by swamps, meadows and occasional Indian clearings in the lowlands."[24] One early description of Dutch-controlled New Netherland (renamed New Jersey under the English) was provided in Holland in 1649:

> *With the exception of the Maize lands, flats and valleys, which have few*
> *or no trees and could with little labor be converted into good tillage land,*

*the soil is commonly covered with all sorts of timber standing, however,
without order as in other wildernesses...The soil...produces several kinds
of timber...consisting of various sorts of oak...; various sorts of Nut
timber...; hickory. This timber is very abundant here, and much used as
firewood...; Chestnuts...; three sorts of Beeches, such as the water-beech,
common beech and hedge beech, axhandle wood, two sorts of canoe wood,
ash, birch, pine lathwood, Imberen or wild cedar, linden, alder, willow,
thorn, elder.*[25]

One major difference in the early settlers' experience with the landscape
has to do with the intimate way in which our colonial ancestors were so
familiar with the natural world. Living face to face with nature on a daily
basis creates a unique attitude toward life and how we live our lives. While
the types of forests that existed in seventeenth and eighteenth century
eastern colonies are somewhat similar to today in terms of species of trees,
their extent or range is vastly changed.[26] And with that change in extent of
forest is a change in perspective of the natural world.

In northern New Jersey, Indian populations were small and consequently
there was little clearing prior to European settlers' arrivals.[27] The Lenni
Lenape, the major tribe in northern New Jersey, "lived in scattered small
hamlets where they grew maize, squashes and other garden crops, and fished
and hunted."[28] They were sparsely settled in the area of northern New Jersey
and at no time did their population exceed eight thousand.

This meant that the forests were little impacted by human activity. It also
meant that a considerable amount of time would be needed to clear land
for agricultural purposes. "With the exception of scattered bogs and a few
Indian old fields the Highlands were forested, and to the first settlers wood
must have seemed inexhaustible."[29] By the time the English gained control
of the colony in 1664, the patterns of settlement and land use were already
being established. The general pattern followed the potential nonagricultural
productivity of the land—that is, exploitation of natural resources. "The
northern highlands were an area in which the pioneers were 'manufacturers
rather than agriculturists,' and where the forge was uniformly the precursor
of the farm."[30]

Northern New Jersey—currently comprising the counties of Sussex,
Passaic, Bergen, Hudson, Essex, Union and Morris—was generally not
as well suited to agriculture as the central and southern portions of the
state were. "Most of the area is characterized by steep slopes, thin and
excessively rocky soils, and, in the recently glaciated northern section, by

many swamps and poorly drained hollows."[31] "From the viewpoint of the settler interested primarily in good farmland, most of the Highlands were decidedly unappealing."[32] This is not to say, of course, that farming did not occur in northern New Jersey. However, based on records and physical land composition, the overall area of northern New Jersey lacked the qualities of seemingly endless agricultural opportunities.

The Highlands themselves "are a narrow, irregular range of hills which extend approximately sixty miles in a northeasterly direction across the northern part of the state from the Delaware River to the boundary of New York."[33] Physically, New Jersey is made up of five distinct areas: (1) outer coastal plain covering much of southern New Jersey; (2) inner coastal plain; (3) piedmont; (4) highlands; and (5) ridge and valley.[34]

It is important to remember that these gradations do not run in a strictly east–west, horizontal pattern, but more diagonally across the state. The area of the highlands, which concerns the iron industry most, is known more formally in geological terms as the "Reading Prong of the New England Upland, so called because the area is an extension of New England's hard crystalline rocks."[35] "The highlands form a belt from about ten to twenty-five miles in width and encompass about one-eighth of the state's total area."[36] (See Appendix E for a more detailed geological depiction of New Jersey.)

HOW THE RESOURCES WERE APPROACHED

As with all regions of the eastern colonies, no one area was totally devoid of other businesses, particularly agriculture. In New Jersey, the highlands and their proximity were no exception. While the area was not completely given over to the iron industry, the vast majority was. Enough agricultural land was necessary to allow for the greater amounts of land given over to iron production to succeed. Even with an iron industry though, food was still a necessity.

Northern New Jersey had an abundance of the three primary ingredients necessary for a successful iron industry: waterpower, wood and ore. Some of the most highly concentrated areas of ore deposits were in the Mount Hope and Hibernia areas—both areas where the Fords ultimately had interests.

The northern part of the state was suited for resource exploitation in the form of iron ore and logging for charcoal.[37] Charcoal was a major component of iron production. During the colonial period, the manufacturing of charcoal iron was widespread in the eastern United States.[38] The New Jersey highlands were representative of the major charcoal iron-producing regions.[39] In northern New Jersey, "the industry developed into a major economic activity which influenced settlement, transportation, the establishment of commercial and other industrial enterprises."[40]

Clearly, the presence of wood, iron ore and waterpower alone did not ensure a successful iron industry. Social and political factors were necessary to ensure the systematic exploitation of the resources. Conditions had to exist to enable the nascent economy to flourish. Lastly, an economic understanding was necessary to create the business model that employed a workforce outside the traditional agricultural sphere.

A ready market was also necessary to ensure an outlet for the items produced by the iron industry. This market may not have always been local either. Some forges were in business to produce iron for the European market, specifically England. This would prove crucial because of "the fact that Britain, as the greatest industrial power of the eighteenth century, could provide the manufactures the Americans wanted and needed far more cheaply than they could be produced in America."[41] Philadelphia also provided a market which was not necessarily local.

This inability to take full advantage of the means of production of the plentiful raw resources available would plague the colonies most dramatically during the Revolution. It would later be one of the great achievements that in the new United States the means of production became comparable with the processing of the raw materials to the point where production to a finished product was feasible. Shipping raw products three thousand miles across an ocean clearly put the colonies at a disadvantage and lead, in some measure, to the imbalance in the cycle of production that emerged as one of the underlying disputes leading to American independence.[42]

New Jersey Agriculture

Besides a burgeoning iron industry, John Ford would have found many traditional family farms in northern New Jersey. In some cases, these farms had coalesced into small communities, such as Morristown. By 1750, when John's son, Jacob Ford Sr., was forty-five, these communities were small and ill defined.

For New Jersey overall, agriculture had played a prominent role. While the founding of every colony had as one of its roots the creation of commodities through farming, New Jersey had particular trouble with producing crops such as fiber crops and silk for naval stores. Hemp and flax were encouraged by the British government, although the colonists in New Jersey seemed "very little if at all acquainted with the proper methods of sewing or curing hemp, or of preparing trees for making tar fit for cordage."[43] As late as 1765, Governor William Franklin was encouraging the growth of "Hemp & Flax" to New Jersey farmers.[44] This approach to farming indicates that some element of the farm industry was a form of business wherein the production of farms was virtually all consumed by nonfood interests rather than producing food for the public.[45]

While food-producing New Jersey farmers had the metropolitan market of New York or Philadelphia in the southern parts of the colony, farming was still a somewhat precarious business during the colonial era and well into the American early national period. Surplus produce had to have an outlet for farmers to survive. With little domestic market (aside from New York or Philadelphia) available, food-producing farmers had to turn overseas for opportunities for their farm products. The same was true in part for fishermen and lumbermen.[46] However, certain items were prohibited from being shipped directly to England in an effort to keep local prices high there. This meant the colonial farmer had to look to other places in Europe and in the Caribbean Islands.[47]

To encourage the marketing of edible farm products, many communities established markets and fairs, often with the support of the colonial government or of the proprietors. In John Ford's town of Woodbridge, one such market was organized in "the old European [style], primarily for the exchange of goods."[48] While these gatherings tended to promote social interaction, not everyone was content with such simple pleasures. Gambling, horse racing and heavy drinking started to plague these events by the mid-eighteenth century.

The American merchant, the engine of economic progress, had a disproportionate impact on northern New Jersey.[49] This was primarily due to the physical characteristics of the land—iron ore deposits, abundant tree and water resources. The farmer, however, was also a part of this mix and cannot be overlooked. Even though the Fords were highly successful in business, they and many like them still had a commercial farm at their Morristown property by 1775 and at some of their earlier homes too.

ANIMALS

In terms of livestock, local efforts were made to protect them from predators. Wolves and panthers were a major threat to farm animals, and as early as 1675, legislation was passed to protect livestock by encouraging hunting of predators with rewards for hides.[50] Livestock was the subject of many pieces of legislation throughout the eighteenth century. This legislation dealt with both the breeding and protection of herds and also individual animals. It was the goal of many of the laws pertaining to livestock to avoid "the introduction of quarrels, disputes, and lawsuits among neighbors."[51] While we do have references to livestock in the wills of most of the Fords, it is not known whether they ever ran afoul of any of the laws designed to protect neighbor from neighbor.

One constant issue involving livestock was the value of the investment in terms of the food necessary to raise the cattle or pigs and the return on that investment. In other words, are the grain foods given to certain types of livestock really cost effective on the surface without government subsides?

In 1818, this question was raised by Estwick Evans:

> *With respect to the raising of cattle too we act…unwisely…According to the limited production of our farms, our cattle are too numerous. We lose one half of the food appropriated for them, by applying it to too great a number. In many cases our cattle are not worth so much in the spring of the year as they were in the preceding fall. Our swine, in particular, are kept poor until the crops come in, and then it costs to fatten them three times as much as they are worth.*[52]

Indeed, if a more equitable approach to the use of grain had existed during the Revolution we might not today be telling stories of the horrible starving that occurred during the war. This imbalance in the cost-benefit ratio in terms of the amount of grain feed necessary to sustain livestock for a relatively small portion of the population is with us to this day.

LABOR

The agricultural business in early eighteenth-century America was a complex system functioning under the notion of freedom of labor, a concept greatly at odds with the practice in seventeenth- and eighteenth-century England.

The idea had its origin as early as 1614 with the writings of Captain John Smith. He saw "work, industry, and enterprise" as the way to make British North America a "heaven for the struggling laborers, tradesman, and small producers of Stuart England."[53] By this argument, only those who controlled their own labor, essentially the small farmer or craftsman, were free.

An employment crisis in England around the mid-seventeenth century led to a major wave of migration from England to the New World. It is not known whether these factors motivated the first Fords to journey to America, but it is known that they set themselves up as small farmers in Massachusetts by about 1660. It's hard to imagine that they were not impacted to some degree by the motivation and desire to control their own labor.

Chapter 2

IRON AND ECONOMICS

THE RISE OF COLONIAL IRON

Among the North American continent's most prized resources, iron ore also proved to be one of the most problematic. From the first days of the settlements in the early seventeenth century by Europeans, iron tools were needed in great abundance by the new arrivals. British merchants and iron producers were not unaware of this need. In fact, they saw a whole new market for their wares.[54]

On April 10, 1608, the first ship loaded with American raw materials, including iron ore, left Jamestown for England.[55] Early reports on the iron in Virginia stated that the ore "had been found to yield as good iron as any in Europe."[56] By 1619, colonists with iron-working skills were specifically sent to Virginia to develop the industry. Captain John Smith wrote, "Who will undertake the rectifying of an iron forge, if those that by meat, drink, coals, ore, and all necessaries at a dear rate gain; where all these things are to be had for the taking up, in my opinion cannot lose."[57] In other words, if nothing else was easy, iron ore was; it could be extracted with minimal effort and forged into a raw product for shipment back to England.[58] Smith exuded optimism, claiming the resources in Virginia, "Free stone for building, Slate for tiling, smooth stone to make furnaces and forges for glass or iron, and iron ore sufficient, conveniently to melt in them."[59] Iron, while not the gold or silver early investors hoped to find in the New World, was from the beginning an important and valuable natural resource in Virginia.

Unfortunately in Virginia, the first attempt at establishing an industry ended after a fierce Indian raid. It is known that the natives used iron in a poor-quality version for hunting and armaments. Perhaps the attack stemmed from a concern of losing more than just their land. This raid also had severe consequences for the iron industry overall in the south. "At the close of the seventeenth century and for some years after the beginning of the eighteenth century New Jersey was the only colony outside of New England that engaged in the manufacture of iron."[60] What distinguished the northern industry from the southern was the ownership of the means of production. In New Jersey and other northern industrial sites, the iron mines and production processes were owned by individual small investors. In the south, particularly in Virginia, the investors in the business owned the mines and the means of production through a company.[61]

Records indicate that the first ironworks in New Jersey were started in 1674, ten years after the British had secured the area from the Dutch.[62] Colonel Lewis Morris, uncle of the royal governor of the same name, was given a grant of land dated October 26, 1676, to "dig, delve, and carry away all such mines for iron as they shall find or see fit to dig and carry away to the iron work."[63] Nearly sixty years after the disastrous events in Virginia, the commitment to an iron industry and the lure of an exploitable natural resource was still a compelling motivation in the mid-Atlantic region. In 1682, eight years after the Lewis Morris grant, an entry was made by the proprietors of East Jersey stating "there is already a smelting furnace and forge set up in this colony, where is made good iron, which is of great benefit to the country."[64]

Limiting the opportunities of colonial iron producers was one way of keeping English investment returns high. Ensuring that the colonists sent the raw product back to England for processing and then reselling finished products back to the colonists ensured a higher return for investors. "In the counting houses of London it seemed first-rate business to restrict the colonials to the production of pig iron [which was shipped to England for processing and re-exported back to America] thereby protecting for British manufacturers the colonial market for British finished products."[65] This approach was separate from the way in which direct investors in the southern colonies operated. The theory was that colonies existed for the benefit of the mother country. Within this theory, individual investors provided huge sums of capital in return for future profits. In the northern colonies, the general approach was that the colony was to benefit the mother country too, but individual investors in the mother country had a much less active role in direct investment.

Prohibitions imposed by England no doubt restricted and retarded the growth of the industry in New Jersey, as opposed to if the colony had been left to establish itself. England, as a colonial power, saw the colonies in terms of enterprise and sought to regulate business with and within the colonies to ensure a favorable return on investments to British investors. Even though the colony was very active during the eighteenth century in terms of iron producing expansion, "restrictions imposed by the mother country" greatly reduced the overall potential.[66]

The need for iron products in America quickly outpaced Britain's ability to supply them in a timely manner. The beginnings of American iron working were therefore as much out of necessity as anything else. Also, the seemingly unlimited supply of natural resources immediately lent itself to the establishment of industries that took advantage of such riches, whether it was the iron industry or any other that depended on natural resources. "An abundance of raw materials, the pressure of skilled labor, the colonials' need for iron at home and exportable goods to trade, and the demand for pig iron in England generated an incentive for the development of furnaces."[67]

This abundance was in part responsible for America's rise in the iron industry irrespective of English motivations. By 1770, "the American colonies had made themselves the world's third largest iron producer."[68] For the nascent American industry, the raw materials equaled prosperity. While the colonies did in fact send large quantities of pig iron (smelted iron ore) to England, enough of a market for pig iron developed internally to ensure a viable outlet for the iron produced in the colonies. "Despite various unenforceable Parliamentary acts prohibiting the manufacture of finished iron products, colonial craftsmen regularly produced" a variety of wares for domestic consumption in contravention of English laws.[69]

How They Functioned

The iron industry quickly adapted European practices to American colonial realities. "Immigrants to America in the seventeenth century brought from Europe knowledge of three basic techniques for making iron: bloom smelting, blast furnace smelting, and fining."[70] Naturally the colonists used the means they knew best. What was unique though in the colonies was the multiplicity of names and terms used from one colony to another or one region from another. "We often have to discover what names meant from context or material evidence."[71]

Furnaces were used to smelt iron ore to create pig iron—the basic, most unworked type of iron manageable. The furnaces were often fired by charcoal made from timber. Most furnace owners, including the Ford's, "owned ore pits and timberlands as well."[72] It was uncommon for producers of pig iron to own the means of further refinement of the iron.[73] The process was very labor intensive and a reliable and knowledgeable work force had to be in place to make the system function.

Workers did not deem allegiance to one owner as something that was necessarily important. Workers moved around at will often changing location when small ore deposits ran out, or mining became too dangerous in individual mines. This led to a more fluid industry in the colonies which helped to produce a much better quality of iron overall due to the cross-pollination achieved by workers relocating. It was work which demanded complete attention from staff to the point of putting the "tending [of] the furnace above personal preferences about work times and methods."[74]

New Jersey Iron

Two Europeans who came to the colonies to pursue their iron business ambitions were Peter Hasenclever and John Jacob Faesch. Hasenclever came to the colonies representing an iron company he had formed in London. He arrived in 1764, two years after Jacob Ford Jr.'s marriage. In what is now Passaic County, he formed the Ringwood mine and enlarged it through purchases of smaller mines in the area. He expanded throughout the county, building furnaces and forges as well as developing the mines. He overextended financially and was forced into bankruptcy in 1770.[75]

His business partner, John Jacob Faesch, who had been with Hasenclever for over five years, took over some of his properties in 1770.[76] Faesch was also involved with Jacob Ford Jr. in business ventures. Ford Jr. leased to Faesch the large farmhouse and property at Mount Hope he had built several years prior to building the mansion in Morristown. Faesch also had built and operated a furnace at Mount Hope.

Faesch was succeeded by Robert Erskine at some of the former Hasenclever properties. Today Erskine is more remembered for producing some of the most accurate topographical maps of the period for the American army during the Revolution.

The Hibernia furnace, in which the Fords had extensive business interests, was quite active during the Revolutionary War. Samuel Ford,

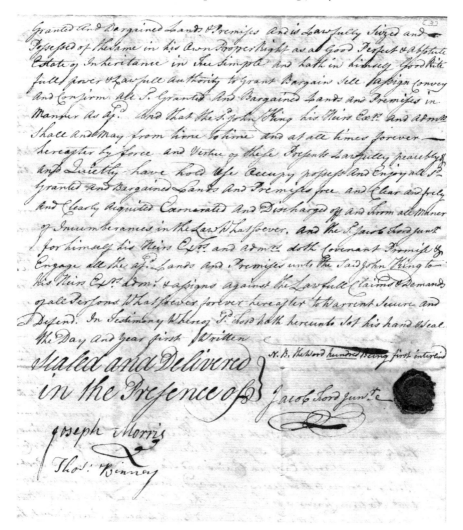

Legal manuscript with signature and seal of Jacob Ford Jr. *Morristown National Historical Park.*

nephew of Jacob Ford Sr., was one of the original investors in the Hibernia mine. In 1765, Samuel Ford sold his portion—not to his relatives—and became a counterfeiter notorious for his skill and ability to evade capture. When he was finally apprehended, he escaped to Virginia, died and entered historical lore.[77]

Along with Hibernia, the forge at Mount Hope was also important to the war effort during the Revolution. By 1777, both the Hibernia and Mount Hope furnaces were "in blast."[78] This was so significant that on October 7,

1777, the New Jersey Provincial Congress passed a law "exempting men to be employed at Mount Hope and Hibernia furnaces from military service" and acknowledging that both sites were heavily involved in producing material needed for the war effort.[79]

A mine at Andover had a similar issue to deal with during the Revolution. The site in question, at one time owned in part by William Penn, was by the outbreak of hostilities owned and operated by Loyalists. Naturally this was a cause for concern. Beyond the loyalties of the owners though, the issue of the quality of the ore and the iron produced in the Andover forge and furnace was something that also could not be overlooked. The Continental Congress, apprised of the situation after the abandonment of the facilities by the owners, in 1778 ordered that the site should be reactivated for the American cause.[80]

The exact list of forges, furnaces and iron mines that the Fords were involved with is hard to discern precisely. Among those which can be linked with the family are Hibernia, Mount Hope, Mount Pleasant, Speedwell pond, Denmark (north of Rockaway) and Middle Forge. Without extensive examination of deeds, record books, letters and journals, it may never be known what exactly they had. Naturally, researching those sources comes with the prerequisite that manuscripts with that information still exist. Assuming research material comes to light, it may also help to further understand the role the Fords played in the iron industry and how extensive their activities were.

Among mines and forges in northern New Jersey during the eighteenth and nineteenth centuries were: Franklin furnace; Union ironworks; Oxford; Sterling; and Ogden.[81] Some of these sites were in business during the mid-eighteenth century and produced cannonballs for the French and Indian War. Much like determining the Ford involvement, identifying all the iron industry-related businesses in New Jersey prior to 1850 would comprise a work unto itself. (See Appendix D for perhaps the most thorough study of Morris County iron mines to date.)[82]

Aside from agriculture, the iron industry provided a much-needed source of revenue for Morris County, and in some instances it created great wealth for a handful of investors and owners, like Jacob Ford Sr. While the process of working with the iron ore was one aspect of the business, the other was the actual management of the process and the byproduct of the process. In certain areas, iron production was quite large; "the iron business in Morris County grew until by the time of the American Revolution there were three blast furnaces in operation and over forty forges."[83] The area along the

View of the Whippany River today at the site of the early John Ford forge. *NPS photo by Krystal Poelstra.*

Whippany River was the focus of the earliest settlements in Morris County due to the nearby gristmills, sawmills and iron forges.[84]

There is evidence that John Ford (grandfather of the builder of the mansion), after relocating from Woodbridge, had a functioning forge in operation by 1715 in the Morris County area, although he was better known as a carpenter as he attests in his will. This was by no means, however, the first forge in New Jersey, as records indicate that the earliest forge in New Jersey operated in the area by 1685.[85] A significant impetus to the iron industry in New Jersey was the passage of the Iron Act of 1750 by the British Parliament. The act removed all duties on pig iron shipped from America to Britain. This act proved tremendously beneficial in supporting the New Jersey industry. While records indicate New Jersey sent relatively little iron overseas by this point, the act nonetheless insured a market should domestic consumption falter.[86]

The early 1740s, when the county was created, coincides with an increase in the number of forges operating in the area. This increase in business no doubt greatly benefited the Ford family. In fact, given the size of his operation, and the accumulating wealth, entrepreneurs like "Jacob Ford [who] were owners of large iron works...hired bloomers and foundry men

County historical marker in Whippany, New Jersey. *NPS photo by Krystal Poelstra.*

and may not themselves have known much about actual iron making."[87] The fact that certain individual owners had businesses large enough to hire staff was significant too. It shows that a labor force could be maintained beyond the self-employment realm. Working for someone, rather than being self-employed, indicates an economy, however small, which can support hired labor in a manufacturing business.

Next to agriculture, the iron industry was infused into every facet of the economic and, thus, the social life in northern New Jersey. The imposing of a business class on the traditional social patterns of agriculture created a societal atmosphere where the contours of money determined the leading citizens. Given the success of their iron business, the Fords clearly enjoyed considerable stature. The extent of their stature is evident in the Morristown mansion; the mansion was not only possible financially but a part of the society, which recognized and understood such displays of wealth. Much like today, a mansion in eighteenth-century America was more than just shelter from the elements; mansions project financial as well as social status; the Fords and their neighbors understood this.

The Morris County area developed much like the surrounding areas in terms of agriculture being the dominating source of income for residents. The iron industry provided a supplement, although it peaked with agriculture during the decade before the Revolution. Morristown could boast a diversified economy, thanks in part to the iron industry, composed of lumber, textile and grain processing.[88] "In addition to iron, magnetite, graphite, mica, limestone and quartz were also mined."[89] "A list of taxable property in the township of Morris in 1779 indicates that the town then featured seven saw mills, six gristmills, four tan yards, and seven forges, but no furnaces."[90] Within Morris County, there were three blast furnaces and over forty forges.[91] (See Appendix A for a more detailed discussion of Morris County iron.)

How the Early Iron Businesses Functioned

Primarily due to the abundance of timber for charcoal, American iron makers were able to continue production the old-fashioned way decades after the British were forced to turn to the use of coal for their forges and furnaces. This shift in a fuel source in England necessitated different types of furnaces due to the heating qualities of the individual fuels.[92]

Many of the early forges were not just setting the trend or example for later forge operations, they were also pioneers in the economic realities that accompanied the founding of the new republic. Much of the history of the iron industry in roughly the first quarter of the nineteenth century is centered on the expansion and consolidation of business practices and the enhancement of the iron processing craft.

The first integrated iron firms (those working from ore to useable consumer products) that owned every aspect of the process, from mining to the marketing, did not appear in America until about 1840.[93] Iron-smelting firms were some of the highest capitalized businesses by the mid-nineteenth century.[94] While at the same time, the industry was beset by a range of maladies ranging from labor issues to frozen ore pits to furnace malfunctions.[95]

Many of the problems that affected the colonial and post-colonial industry were attributable to the overall development process not just of iron but of business practices in general.[96] Support infrastructures had not yet been developed to ensure more predictable functioning of a particular industry from raw production to the finished product's sale. A banking system capable of providing credit and financing products was necessary to ensure a ready supply of capital, and this did not exist. "The ordinary medium of exchange among the colonists was bills of credit, so disadvantageous because of their fluctuating and usually deteriorated values."[97]

PROBLEMS WITH IRON

Like most areas of heedless exploitation, the highlands suffered from overabundance of enthusiasm and ambition on the part of land speculators.[98] Even though laws were in place by 1666 to protect timber from being cut on unpatented land or land that was still held by the proprietors, in practice these laws had little effect.

As with any economy based too extensively on natural resources, there was always the possibility of depleting those resources and thus jeopardizing the economic foundation. This was in danger of happening; "By the late 1700s in New Jersey, considerable depletion of natural resources had occurred."[99] Several decades into the nineteenth century, the situation was even worse.

Although forges lingered on until after the Civil War, it was clear from an early date that the rate of production in the iron industry was unsustainable. Writing in the late eighteenth century, a German naturalist noted:

> *The business of the mines and foundries in New Jersey as well as throughout America, cannot be said to be on as firm a basis as in most parts of Europe, because nobody is concerned about forest preservation, and without an uninterrupted supply of fuel and timber, many works must go to ruin, as indeed has already been the case here and there. Not the least economy is observed with regard to forests. The owners of furnaces and foundries possess for the most part great tracts of appurtenant woods, which are cut off, however, without system or order.*[100]

In fact, a New Jersey state report from 1889 concluded that, by 1850, deforestation for the purposes of the iron industry left large swaths of former timberland in a condition that "presented a perfectly bare appearance."[101]

IMMIGRANT

By 1700, around the year John Ford arrived in New Jersey, "some 155,000 immigrants from England, Ireland, and Scotland [had] arrived in the mainland colonies."[102] The majority of these were indentured servants; the Fords were not among the indentured class. "New Jersey possessed the most culturally diverse population of the entire area at an early time, with distinct contrasts in the regional concentrations of some of the cultural groups."[103] One of the primary reasons for this was New Jersey's location between two of the most important cities in North America: New York and Philadelphia. "New Jersey received population and culture from both these hearths."[104]

What drove John Ford to leave Massachusetts and ultimately Connecticut for New Jersey at the end of the seventeenth century is not completely clear. There is evidence that one of the earliest ironworks in New Jersey was started by immigrants from Connecticut with the name of Leonard. While it is supposition, John Ford may have known about this and consciously made the decision to relocate to New Jersey for this reason.[105] Whatever the motivation, this move precipitated the rise of one of the most important families in eighteenth-century New Jersey. By 1715, after only about fifteen years in the colony, John Ford had established a forge at Hanover, the site of present-day Whippany, and was quickly becoming a major landowner. Court records indicate extensive buying and selling of real estate by John Ford. From the early beginnings of John Ford, the involvement of the Ford family in the New Jersey iron industry tracked nearly exactly the lifespan of the industry itself within New Jersey.

FORD BEGINNINGS

To what extent John Ford and his son, Jacob Ford Sr., fashioned themselves as businessmen is not known.[106] Did they have the same sense of the business world that we today associate with those who devote their entire being to financial reward? Colonial businessmen and the attitude toward the concept of business was not necessarily the same in terms of concepts and understandings as today. As investors in the iron industry as opposed to hands-on workers, the Fords still probably never saw themselves as venture capitalists.

The pace of business was clearly slower than today. "There were scarcely any specializing institutions or individuals."[107] Business systems, "documents as well as procedures," were not standardized, creating needless confusion and difficulty.[108] The Fords in the early years must have relied on their own sense of managing to a certain degree when they were beginning the business. The overwhelming need for iron products though would have ensured the Fords a ready market for quality material.

By all available evidence, the Fords remained purely regional in their practices, which moved the industry through the eighteenth century. This makes them not unusual with other New Jersey producers. By 1825, however, the industry was increasingly dominated by huge proto-corporations that would fuel the American Industrial Revolution.[109]

What this meant was that the Fords probably did not function as later nineteenth century "captains of industry," owning every aspect of a resource—from raw to finished product. The Fords oversaw one aspect of the process, which is in keeping with the general pattern for colonial businessmen. The infrastructure simply did not exist in colonial America for large-scale ownership of an entire industry. "Adequate supervision required continual attendance on the grounds, and the limited number of owners, together with slow transportation, discouraged single-firm ownership of several geographically separated" areas of production.[110] The types of operations run by the Fords required heavily on family networks to maintain smooth management. Extended family involvement also helped to reduce but not eliminate the already high number of lawsuits.

Part 2

Last Will and Testament

The story of how the Fords distributed their legacy is really the heart of the matter in terms of their family dynamics. Because of this, discussion in this work on the written legacies is taking place in the center. It was their wills that set the foundations of the family and provided the spirit to keep their drive in motion. For over 150 years, the family charted their progress and status through reflection at the end of each member's life. For us today, this practice they kept allows us to peer ever so slightly into their private lives. Whether they intentionally destroyed their private papers or whether time took its toll, their wills have fortunately withstood the decades.

Chapter 3

THE FORDS OF NEW JERSEY

THE FAMILY: AN OVERVIEW

Family trees are always difficult. Generations recycle names among both male and female members; births and deaths are not always recorded; and people move and lose touch with their relatives. The Fords of New Jersey (no relation to the auto king Henry Ford or President Gerald Ford) are no exception to this trend.

Surviving records indicate that John Ford migrated to eastern New Jersey from New England and arrived around 1701. New Jersey at the time was divided between East and West Jersey, an archaic holdover from the seventeenth-century approach to land distribution.[111] The system itself was a holdover from even more archaic land distribution practices of the Middle Ages. The colony, while divided geographically, was however unified for political purposes two years later, when it was denoted as one colony under Queen Anne in 1702. While this approach to governing consolidated governmental efforts, the colony for all practical purposes was still two areas. The east and west approached life from very different points of view.

The west never experienced the sometimes violent arguments over land ownership that existed in the east. While no one reason for this exists, one must surely be the approach to land ownership among the population and the attitudes of the two sets of proprietors to property rights. The east had a much more feudal, aristocratic application, as opposed to the west. "The great number of Quakers in the western division accounts in part for this discrepancy."[112]

Industrial east Jersey outproduced and outnumbered by population the more agrarian west. This is not to say, however, that agriculture was not the primary way of life for East Jersey residents. It did, in contrast to the west, have an element of industry and commerce that allowed a small number of residents to thrive well beyond their neighbors. The Fords were one such family that did thrive. Perhaps they did not thrive so much immediately when John Ford arrived in the early eighteenth century, but it was not long after. John Ford established the family in the iron business by about 1710–1715, and the family would prosper from this move for well over 150 years.

THE FORD FAMILY MEMBERS AND THEIR WRITTEN LEGACIES

The keeping of a last will and testament is a practice for which the originating idea is long forgotten. Wills naturally provided a means to transfer assets after one's death. Wills existed both informally and formally throughout much of recorded history. Whether by the verbal pronouncements of the testator or through some unwritten custom or tradition whereby property descended by right, assets have changed hands among generations as long as anyone can document.

By the eighteenth century, a much more formal practice of asset transfer after death existed in Western Europe that was transplanted to the colonies. We associate wills during the colonial period with wealth or at least with those individuals with enough assets to pass on requiring written instruction. While it is always hazardous to speculate on terms inferring societal class status, it is nonetheless a fair characterization to ascribe to those individuals in the "upper" class as having more genuine need for a written last will and testament. Naturally, men in this class were more likely than women to possess such documents, as their wills generally included instructions for the assets pertaining to their widows. Bearing this in mind, the Fords were in some respects typical of the period, and in some, not so typical. The wealth and extensive business dealings of the family clearly necessitated a will to ensure an equitable maintenance of the family assets. The Fords were responsible stewards of their holdings. There is no indication that they thought otherwise.

The wills of John Ford, Jacob Ford Sr., Jacob Ford Jr., Gabriel and Henry are fascinating for the way they chart the progression of the family. It can be seen over the course of more than a century how the family grew in business and in the networks along with a business perspective and from the familial side. It was not just the male line who kept wills either. Hannah and Theodosia, wives of Jacob Sr. and Jacob Jr. respectively, also had wills. Unfortunately, the wills of Ford Sr. and Ford Jr. are too close in time to really chart any outstanding difference, although the hastiness with which Ford Sr. rewrote his will to account for Ford Jr.'s death is telling. Each family member's last will and testament will be examined shortly in their individual sections of this chapter. The Ford family members will be introduced through their last will and testament as a way to open ever so slightly a view on their collective understanding of their responsibilities to the concept of family, work and the development of an identity. One compelling aspect of the wills of the first three Ford men is that they all mention a specific two-hundred-acre plot of land. While not clearly identified, this is probably the two hundred acres that Jacob Sr. gave to Jacob Jr. upon the latter's marriage in 1762 to Theodosia

Henry Augustus Ford, circa 1855. He was the last Ford to own the mansion. *Genealogical and Memorial History of the State of New Jersey.*

Historical plaque in the First Presbyterian Church in Morristown indicating the location and brief life stories of Jacob Ford Sr., Jacob Ford Jr. and Theodosia Ford. *NPS photo by Krystal Poelstra.*

Johnes. The two hundred acres Ford Sr. deeded to his son in 1762 was well above the average for a farm in the Morristown area, which was around one hundred and twenty five acres.[113] And, the two hundred acres was only a fraction of Ford Sr.'s overall holdings. Jacob Ford Sr. had provided his son upon his marriage to the daughter of the rector of the Presbyterian church an estate of considerable size. This may also explain why Jacob Jr. decided to build his mansion on this site given its family legacy history.

JOHN FORD OF WOODBRIDGE (C.1675–1721/22)

The John Ford of the early eighteenth century came from Weymouth, Massachusetts, and was born around 1675, the son of James Ford. John had moved to Windham, Connecticut, and was formally admitted as an inhabitant on December 12, 1698. Less than three years later, on November, 12, 1701, John Ford lost his land in Windham by judgment of the Inferior Court at Hartford and immediately moved to Woodbridge, New Jersey. Here he married Elizabeth Freeman on December 18, 1701. It seems odd that he moved to a

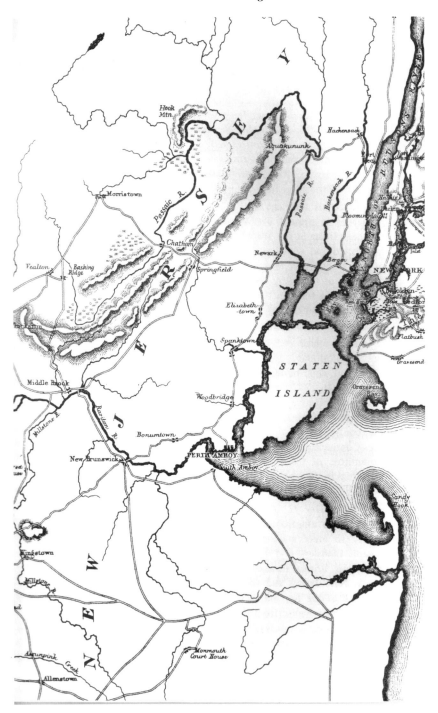

Early map of New Jersey showing Woodbridge across from Staten Island. Woodbridge was where John Ford first settled in New Jersey. *Morristown National Historical Park.*

new colony and within a month is married—but the records indicate this. Elizabeth Freeman lived until age ninety-one, dying in 1772, the same year her grandson, Jacob Jr., started to build his mansion in Morristown.[114]

John Ford was a carpenter and a miller. In January 1715 (around the same time he was operating a forge in Whippany), a Newark town meeting resolved that "John Fford [sic] should have Liberty to sett up a Mill below ye old mill, and that he should have a Quarter of an acre of Land."[115] He was prosperous enough to become a sizeable landowner before his death in 1722. Surviving deeds show John Ford was quite active in land dealings. Over a roughly twenty-year period, he bought and sold several hundred acres in northern New Jersey. John Ford was also active in his church, being a deacon and a ruling elder by 1710. Additionally he served as justice of the peace for Woodbridge in 1719, starting a tradition of public service that both his son and grandson continued.

John Ford's first son in his growing young family was Jacob, born April 12, 1705, in Woodbridge. Jacob Ford became one of the most influential local men in both business and civic affairs. This Jacob Ford is better known today as Ford Sr., being the father of Jacob Ford Jr., builder of the mansion in Morristown.[116]

John Ford died over the winter of 1721–1722, leaving a will dated October 1721. The will in part reads: "I John Ford of Hanno[over] in the county of Hunterdon and Provience of New Jersey Carpenter [leave 200 acres to my son Jacob in Hanover] likewise all my Lands Lying at Windom above New Norrdig and Likewise that Lyes at Quene bog up New London River that falls to me by my father."[117]

John Ford's will primarily deals with land bequests. There is no mention of iron, equipment, high financial concerns or anything that would indicate wealth in John Ford's will, other than the simple fact that he had one. The main asset is land, left to his two sons, Samuel and Jacob. He appoints his wife, Elizabeth, unique itself, as executor jointly with his associate Josiah Ogden. John Ford was either too ill or incapable of signing his name to his will as he signed with an X for his signature.

Jacob Ford Sr. (1705–1777)

Jacob Ford Sr. married Hannah Baldwin in 1724, two years after the death of his father. Virtually no record of Ford Sr. exists prior to his marriage to Hannah in 1724. After his marriage, "he becomes prominent as one of the

Marker over the grave of Jacob Ford Sr. *NPS photo by Krystal Poelstra.*

pioneers in New Jersey as a landowner, merchant, and iron manufacturer."[118] Jacob Sr. operated a tavern/inn and a store, in addition to his work as a mine owner and public servant. While little direct information exists about Jacob Sr. as an iron-industry businessman, the indirect information clearly indicates an extensive involvement. From 1740 until before his death, he was a judge of the county court, thus perhaps providing a reason why "Esq." is sometimes attached to his name.[119] One of his last major contributions to the colony was as a member of the Provincial Congress that formed at the very early stages of the American Revolution.

The Will

While no doubt still grieving the loss of his principal heir, the untimely death of his son required a quick rewrite of his will. Jacob Ford Sr.'s will is dated January 15, 1777, four days after the death of Jacob Jr. and just a few days before his own. The will was probably made to replace one he had drawn earlier that would have included bequests and instructions to Jacob Jr., his major business partner, now unnecessary. Evidence of the importance that the Fords knew a will would provide to the surviving members of the family can be gleaned from Ford Sr.'s action in rewriting his own. It is also evidence of the litigious environment that permeated eighteenth century colonial business life. Given the inexactitude of land surveys, the fluctuating currency and the slowness of communication, a law court was the likely venue for most disputes that could not be solved amicably. Even within families, particularly those involved in business, lawsuits were all too common.

The two Jacob Fords were more than father and son. They worked closely together as businessmen and both were active in the local political affairs of the community. When the Morristown mansion was built by Jacob Jr., his father and mother were part of the larger family that would consider the mansion as home. The relationship then went beyond just being related; their whole approach to life, business and relationships was intertwined in a way rarely seen today. No other generation of Fords had such a connection between two generations.

Jacob Sr. appointed not his wife or daughter-in-law as his father did as executor but rather business associates. His executors were given wide authority over his business interests and this would lead to legal problems in the near future—particularly with his daughter's husband, Moses Tuttle.

The language of the will was typical of the period with homage to God and an acknowledgement of his mortality. The first bequest is to his wife, Hannah. A cash payment of £1,000 is made, a considerable sum in 1777 at the beginning of a war.[120] Bequests of land were delineated by reference to physical landmarks as opposed to survey boundaries. Jacob Sr. refers to land he inherited from his father John as a way to help establish a lineage and as a way to help further identify often murky boundary lines.

An unusual aspect of Ford Sr.'s will was that it lacked any mention of the iron business. There was a clear attempt to leave the entire estate to family members, but what that estate was comprised of was not mentioned. Perhaps this was an indication of how hastily his will was rewritten. Perhaps it was too difficult to fathom not having his son available to handle the business interests. Or, it simply was felt that it was not necessary to mention it in detail. The reason may never be known. The estate is simply denominated between real and personal property without any further explanation.

HANNAH FORD (1701–1777)

Hannah Ford, widow of Jacob Ford Sr., died in the summer of 1777. She was the fourth and final immediate family member who died in 1777. She was preceded by her son, husband and granddaughter.[121]

Marker over the grave of Hannah Ford. *NPS photo by Krystal Poelstra.*

Hannah Ford's will is dated February 6, 1777, less than a month after the deaths of her son and husband and she refers to herself as "widow of Jacob Ford Esq." Whether she had a will prior to their deaths is unknown. If she had, their combined loss would have necessitated redrawing hers to take in account their deaths. However, she may have drafted her will fresh only after having first seen the provisions of her husband's will as it related to her family's legacy in terms of the female Fords.

The second clause, relating to the women in the family, is probably the most eye-opening for the attitude she takes toward the redistribution of her late husband's estate. It also indicates the will may have been produced for the first time, rather than a rewrite.

> *Whereas my deceased husband did in and by his last will and testament give and devise unto the children of my deceased sons John and Jacob a much greater proportion of his estate than he gave to his daughters—in order therefore to do equal justice to them all, as well as from the affection which I bear to my children I hereby give, devise and bequeath unto my*

Jacob Ford Sr., Hannah Ford, Jacob Ford Jr. and Theodosia Ford, with other Ford family members in the First Presbyterian Church cemetery in Morristown. *NPS photo by Krystal Poelstra.*

daughters Phoebe Phillips, Sarah Tuthill, Mary Dunham, and Jane Tuttle all my estate real and personal to be equally divided between them share and share alike to have and to hold.

Whether this is an early version of "women's power" or not is debatable. But it should be remembered in context that New Jersey's first state constitution in 1776 extended the right to vote to women. Perhaps her move was not that radical seen in this context of New Jersey politics. How radical it was within the Ford family though is unknown. The New Jersey legislature rescinded that right to vote for women in 1807, and women lost the right to vote until 1920 with the passage of the Nineteenth Amendment to the United States Constitution.

JACOB FORD JR. (1738–1777)

Besides his father, Jacob Ford Jr. was by far the most prominent member of the family at the outbreak of the American Revolution.[122] In politics, business and in the rising radicalism of relations with England, Ford Jr. was

Marker over the grave of Jacob Ford Jr. *NPS photo by Krystal Poelstra.*

an influential figure in Morristown and the surrounding area. The building of the Morristown mansion created the visual symbol of the family's power, while his work for the patriot cause set an example that his family would remember with pride for centuries.

In 1776, the year before he died, the Provincial Congress approved a loan of £2,000 for Ford Jr. to build and operate a black powder mill on the Whippany River to supply the Continental army. The British were not unaware of this mill and made no secret of their wishes to attack it—although they never did.[123]

His death in January 1777, at the age of thirty-nine, was a tremendous blow to his family and to his comrades. The elegiac statement on his tombstone reads: "In vain we strive with human skill to avoid the shaft of death; Heaven's high decree it must fulfill and we resign out breath. The friends who read our tomb and mourn and weep our early fall must be lamented in their day and share the fate of all."[124]

There was no typical descent of property between Ford Sr. and Ford Jr. through inheritance upon the death of the father. Since their deaths were nearly simultaneous, they had their lives together during which they continued to advance the work that John Ford started in iron and real estate.

View of the Whippany River today at the site of the early John Ford forge. *NPS photo by Krystal Poelstra.*

"An Easy and Comfortable Life"

Jacob Jr.'s will bears the date July 1, 1776, a month and year that every American is taught to celebrate. Whether Jacob Jr. knew what was transpiring ninety miles away in Philadelphia on July 1 when he signed his will is unknown. But the fact that he felt the need, at thirty-six, to write his will in the midst of a growing armed conflict is telling. As a soldier in an army fighting the largest military force in the world, he perhaps sensed his mortality more than usual. Although there was no mention of the conflict with Great Britain, he clearly felt it prudent to draft his will, given his active involvement and reduced life expectancy. His will was the most important in terms of the family business.

The first clause clearly contains the essence of the will and of the family business activities. Jacob Jr. was involved in numerous business ventures in 1776 and was actively involved in transactions that were quite fluid. He directed his executors—his business partners—to sell those properties necessary to cover any outstanding debts that may exist at the time of his death. Jacob Jr.'s executors were: his "honored" father Jacob Ford Sr.; his father-in-law, the Reverend Timothy Johnes (who is removed from that position by Jacob

Sr.'s redrawn will in 1777 and replaced by Azariah Dunham, his son-in-law); Moses Tuttle, his brother-in-law; and Samuel Tuthill, another brother-in-law. His father, Jacob Sr., must have been in good health in July 1776 when he was appointed an executor, and there must have been a rapid decline by January 1777 when he died.

Jacob Jr.'s will identifies him as the owner of forges in the area and as an active participant in the iron industry in New Jersey. He lists "mountain or rough lands" recently purchased and lists forges at Long Meadow and Middle Forge. Both properties were listed as coming from his father in 1773. Ford Jr. held the properties jointly with Moses Tuttle, husband of his sister, Jane. The Fords leased out both forges and the associated property and as such were owners rather than actual hands-on workers in the business. They participated purely as investors.

Jacob Jr. sought to provide for both his mother and wife in a way any son or husband would. What made his bequests unique was the resources that he had available with which to provide for them. During her life, his mother was to have shelter in the "dwelling house," as Jacob Jr. refers to the mansion, and "such privileges and advantages as she may" need to be provided by the estate.

Jacob Jr. was conscious of the two hundred acres of land deeded to him by his father in 1762 at the time of his marriage to Theodosia Johnes. In fact, the two hundred acres as mentioned earlier was land that probably started with John Ford and as such it had significant family value. The land was to provide, if nothing else existed, all the necessary requirements of life for his descendants. The rents from the leases of forges and associated lands and buildings were separate and liable to not be adequate to provide depending on business circumstances.

To his wife, Theodosia, Jacob Jr. provides much the same types of bequests as with his mother. Theodosia Ford was to have residence in the dwelling house until the eldest son reached twenty one. After which time she could only have use of "the west Part of my house from the middle of the Hall upwards to the top of the House and what cellar room she may want." What was to happen to the east side is unknown, particularly since she was prohibited from leasing any part of the house "to any person whatsoever." The prohibition did not however apply to his sons. The issue became moot anyway, as Jacob Jr.'s son Gabriel made the mansion his permanent residence, thereby ensuring a life home for his mother.

It is interesting to speculate on how Mrs. Ford saw this clause when George Washington arrived to take up residence during the winter encampment of

Mrs. Ford's room during the Washington occupancy of 1779–1780. The room was the dining room of the mansion. *Morristown National Historical Park.*

Bedroom in the west portion of the Ford mansion shared by General and Mrs. Washington during the 1779–1780 winter encampment. *Morristown National Historical Park.*

1779–1780. During Washington's stay, Mrs. Ford was not ensconced in the west side of the mansion, but rather the east. This was probably because Mrs. Ford wanted George and Martha to have the use of the master bedroom, which is in the west portion of the mansion.

The most personal and unique clause, given the absolute silence in the historical record of the personal side of the Ford family, is the third from the last and is not part of the standard language employed at the time. The clause reads "I order my executors out of my Estate to give to my Wife & Daughters & to each of my sisters a genteel Gold Mourning Ring." Whether this occurred is unknown, but it offers an exceedingly rare glimpse into the private feelings of the Ford family.

For his sons, Jacob Jr. wanted his wife to provide a "good liberal education," while for his daughters, he wanted the "best English education." He also desired his children to be taught "Latin," unless his wife objected. He also leaves his "wearing apparel" to his sons, at the discretion of his wife. The residuary part of his estate was to be divided equally between his children, "share and share alike."

THEODOSIA FORD (1741–1824)

Theodosia Ford's will bears the date of April 26, 1823.[125] In it, she gives little hint as to what involvement she may have had in managing the family business. Fortunately, the historical record yields some insight through the few manuscripts that survived besides her will. She gives no personal bequests such as her husband, Ford Jr., made regarding the mourning ring. In fact, it was a very straight forward document of barely one page in length.

She began by directing that her "worldly estate, whatsoever and wheresoever" be divided in four equal parts. One fourth to be given to her eldest son Timothy of Charleston, South Carolina, and another fourth to her son Gabriel of Morristown, who lived with his family and his mother in the mansion.

Another fourth goes to Henry De Saussure, her widower son-in-law in Columbia, South Carolina. The money was to be held in trust to be divided equally among the children of Henry and Mrs. Ford's "deceased and beloved daughter Elizabeth." Finally, the remaining fourth was given to her youngest son Jacob, also of Charleston, South Carolina. Lastly, Mrs. Ford names her grandson Henry A. Ford as executor.

The will lacks specific bequests, and no mention of what her "worldly estate" constituted. There was also no mention of the iron industry, and

Above: Marker over the grave of Theodosia Ford with inscription as designed by Henry Ford. *NPS photo by Krystal Poelstra.*

Right: Instructions by Henry Ford on wording for his grandmother Theodosia's grave marker. *Morristown National Historical Park.*

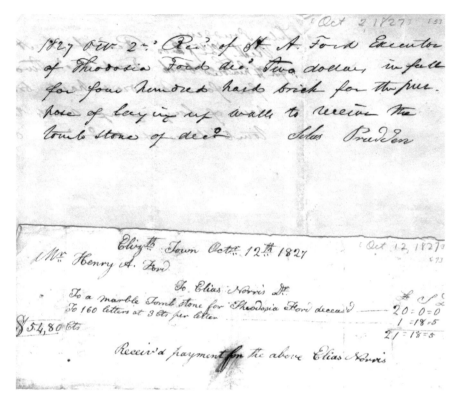

Invoice and receipt for the grave marker and lettering for Theodosia Ford's grave. *Morristown National Historical Park.*

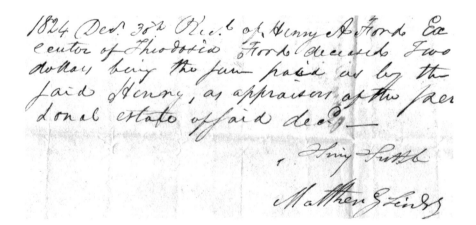

Receipt of Henry Ford for paying appraisers to appraise the estate of his deceased grandmother Theodosia. The appraisal is not known to have survived. *Morristown National Historical Park.*

Last Will and Testament

Letter of Henry Ford to his uncle William De Saussure in South Carolina relating to the settlement of his grandmother Theodosia's estate. *Morristown National Historical Park.*

Invoice for legal work by Henry Ford as executor on his grandmother Theodosia's estate. *Morristown National Historical Park.*

Left: Certified copy of the will of Theodosia Ford. *Morristown National Historical Park.*

Below: Order to Silas Millen, carpenter, for a mahogany coffin for Theodosia Ford at a cost of twenty dollars. *Morristown National Historical Park.*

aside from the reference to her beloved daughter, the will is quite devoid of nearly all personal or emotional language. Theodosia's will was much less fascinating in terms of family dynamics than her mother-in-law Hannah's will fifty years earlier. Hannah's will as remembered had provisions to redistribute financially what she saw as disproportionate bequests to the male Ford line in her late husband Jacob Sr.'s will.

Settling the Estate

Bringing closure to the "worldly estate, whatsoever and wheresoever" it was to be found was not always an easy task.[126] Even with a seemingly straightforward will like Mrs. Ford's, there were issues involved with making sure everything was carried out accurately and with proper accounting.

By all accounts the settlement went smoothly, with one exception. Mrs. Ford held a bond against Moses Phillips for over $5,000.[127] The bond against Phillips concerned the Mount Hope properties, although the specific connection was not elaborated on in the surviving manuscript.

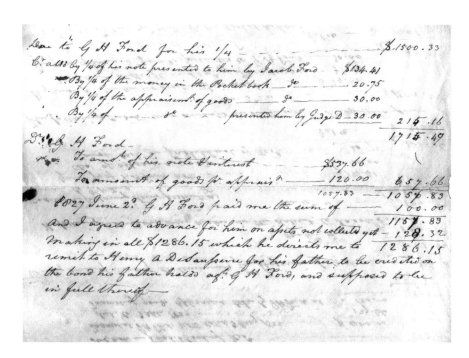

Partial account reconciliation by Henry Ford concerning his grandmother Theodosia's estate. *Morristown National Historical Park.*

Letter from Henry Ford to Moses Phillips inquiring about a bond by Theodosia Ford against Phillips and relating to the settlement of her estate. *Morristown National Historical Park.*

Case of Theodosia Ford deceased versus Moses Phillips. *Morristown National Historical Park.*

Last Will and Testament

Nearly two years after Mrs. Ford's death, her executor, Henry Ford, would write to Moses Phillips in exasperation, "this is the only debt, I think that will prevent my applying to the next…court in September for final settlement."

Problems

In July 1826—nearly two years after Mrs. Ford died—Henry Ford was involved in a lawsuit to obtain the money that had not been paid to the estate relating to the outstanding bond. The bond cost Phillips 7 percent annually and Henry offered to restructure the bond at 6 percent if a reasonable portion were paid off first. This did not happen.

On June 30, 1826, Phillips wrote to Henry Ford from Mount Hope that he could not discuss the pending lawsuit against him. It appears that the issue at

Letter from Henry Ford to Moses Phillips concerning the difficulties Phillips is causing by not paying his bond to the estate of the Theodosia Ford. *Morristown National Historical Park.*

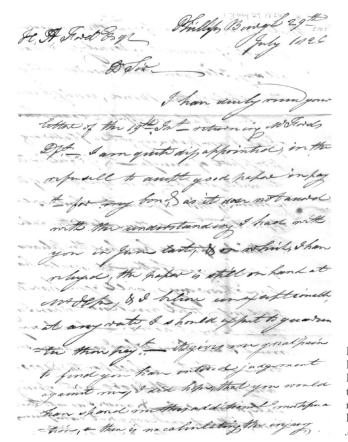

Letter of Gabriel
Ford to Moses
Phillips referencing
the estate of his
mother Theodosia
Ford. *Morristown
National Historical Park.*

Mount Hope dealt with iron interests and that Phillips was trying to secure a buyer to cover his debt to Mrs. Ford. He feels a judgment against him could damage his chances for the sale before it was completed. Phillips asks Henry to persuade his father, Gabriel, to "extend that spirit of accommodation to me." Whether this referred to Gabriel's work as a judge is not known. If so, and Phillips's case was before Gabriel's court and this business relationship existed, Gabriel should no doubt have recused himself.

A week later, on July 7, Phillips wrote that he was enclosing $100 as a deposit on the sum due (Henry rejects it and returns it to Phillips). He was concerned his efforts to sell may be undercut by a judgment against him. "I hope and trust there has been no judgment entered against me, as it will injure my prospects of selling." He promises that even if the sale falls through, he would be able to pay $1,000 by the spring of 1827—providing no judgment be entered against him.

Calculations concerning the Moses Phillips bond. *Morristown National Historical Park.*

Henry Ford's letter on July 19 to Phillips indicates that he was most concerned about that portion of the estate's proceeds going to his relatives in South Carolina. They were to be paid mainly from the money from the bond that Phillips held. "I have given the heirs in South Carolina to understand, long ago, that this estate would have been settled before this time for the collection of all the debts. They expected it, and when they find it not settled the blame will rest with me."[128]

Several weeks later, at the end of July 1826, Phillips wrote again to Henry Ford. "I am greatly disappointed in the refusal to accept good paper in payment for my bond." Henry Ford had rejected the money outright sent earlier in the month as a deposit. Furthermore, Phillips lost the lawsuit filed by Henry Ford on behalf of his grandmother's estate. "It gives me [Phillips] great pain to find you have entered judgment against me. I did hope that you would have spared me the additional [?], there is no calculating the injury that I may sustain from this measure." Phillips continues that he will somehow pay $1,000 later in the summer and $1,000 in the spring of 1827. That is all he could possibly hope to afford.

According to the letters printed in note 128 (at the end of this work), Phillips did lose his property, and through various means, Henry Ford was

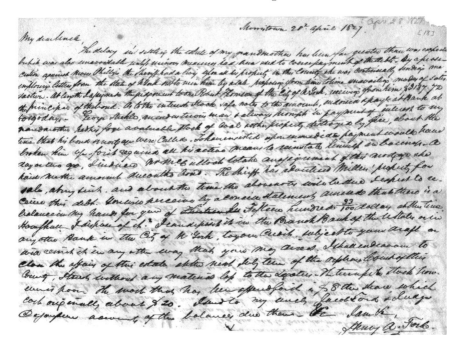

A detailed letter from Henry Ford to his uncle in South Carolina explaining the circumstances surrounding the delays in settling his grandmother's estate. *Morristown National Historical Park.*

able to secure payment through resale of the bond and therefore pay his relatives in South Carolina.

The unfortunate saga relating to the settlement of Mrs. Ford's will indicates that she was involved with financial matters that related directly or indirectly to the iron industry. Whether these were interests carried over from her husband's estate is not known (although they probably were). In any event, the fact was she did have exposure as a businesswoman to the quickly developing world of American finance in the early decades of the nineteenth century to the extent that her estate needed legal assistance to process her bequests.

GABRIEL FORD (1765–1849)

The nineteenth century history of the family is dominated by the figures of Gabriel Ford and his son Henry. Gabriel, the second eldest child of Jacob Jr. and Theodosia, graduated from Princeton in 1784 and became an attorney in 1789. He had a distinguished legal career serving as a judge on the Morris County Court of Common Pleas, and from 1820 to 1840 as a justice on the New Jersey Supreme Court. Much like his parents, Gabriel seems to have not been overly involved in the social atmosphere of the Morristown area. There are no stories or reports of the family being the socialites of Morristown. Society life of any type was not for Gabriel Ford; he did not even feel colleges were suitable places. His sons attended private academies before being tutored by Gabriel in the law.[129]

Gabriel acted as the Ford family attorney, overseeing the family's business and agricultural interests. He kept the long-standing family business interest in the Hibernia mine profitable, and he litigated numerous land disputes involving his father's executors and land connected to the forges. The disputes between the Ford family and other mine operators took on an even more serious tone set against the backdrop of the overall decline of the industry in New Jersey. With their livelihood being threatened by the large iron reserves in the Great Lakes region within the first quarter of the nineteenth century, the last thing New Jersey mine owners needed was internecine legal battles. The iron industry, once the bedrock of northern New Jersey's prominence, was overtaken by cheaper iron produced in the new lands opening in the west, and naturally this produced stress within families.

With the further decline of the iron industry, the Fords—Theodosia; Gabriel; his wife, Frances; and their children—shifted the emphasis more and more to the farming ventures, investments in new modes of transportation like railroads and most noticeably, to the service sector—specifically the legal aspect—of the family business. Gabriel had a lucrative legal career that helped to supplement the declining revenue from the iron industry. Gabriel also took full advantage of the developing investment interests that were quickly appearing after 1800.[130] What remained of the family iron business was increasingly being run by other family members and effectively ceased being a major interest or source of income for the children of Ford Jr. by about 1830.

The financial depression of 1837, one of the most severe national financial crises, would have also played some negative role in the restructuring of the commercial business related ventures of the Fords. At the time, the depression was one of the reasons why President Martin Van Buren was defeated for a second term in 1840. By no means destitute though, the family under Gabriel moved beyond the early industrial generators of wealth (iron) and into the service sector (law, investments) as the Fords deftly learned to accommodate and manipulate the larger commercial and industrialization trends of the state of New Jersey during the mid-nineteenth century.

Gabriel Ford's Investments

Among the many papers relating to the settlement of the estate of Gabriel Ford are examples of the types of investments he made.[131] Looking to the future, he was aware that new technologies would have to be part of a portfolio. A survey reveals paperwork dealing with the disposition by his executor of six mortgage bonds of the New York and Erie Railroad, and six bonds of the Pittsburgh Railroad Company, each worth $1,000. Gabriel's son Henry A. Ford, as executor, sells the bonds for the benefit of the estate. By the terms of Gabriel's will, this move could only be initiated by the executor upon the permission of Gabriel's widow, Frances. As another example of the Fords keeping their business within the family, Frances Ford, of course, happens to be executor Henry Ford's mother. In the specific document dated July 29, 1850, Frances Ford grants permission for the sale, with another Ford, Louisa A. Ford, acting as witness.

By 1852, the estate was divesting itself of more bonds, this time of Cleveland and Pittsburgh Railroad Company. Henry Ford's brothers and one of his sisters sign as relevant family members per their father's will.

Settling his father Gabriel's estate was not always easy. Henry Ford needed to persuade at times: "May I beg you to remit to me by draft on New York [Bank], along with the interest due, a portion of the principle and you will much oblige [me]." *Morristown National Historical Park.*

Request for sale of six bonds of New York Rail Road Company and six bonds of Pittsburgh Railroad Company—totaling $12,000. It was signed by Frances Ford, widow of Gabriel Ford, 1850. *Morristown National Historical Park.*

Their mother, Frances Ford, widow of Gabriel, was too ill and infirm to sign in September 1852 when the document was drafted. Frances Ford died two months later in November 1852.

In December 1852, Henry Ford wrote a letter to one of his debtors concerning land the Fords still held at Hibernia involving iron mines. In an interesting statement, Henry Ford alludes to the timing of the sale relative to the family's overall business intent. Henry Ford writes, "I think the time has arrived when it [the mine] may be safely sold to advantage." As has been discussed, the New Jersey iron industry was greatly reduced by 1850 from what it had been just fifty years earlier. The Fords were increasingly moving into other investments—as is noted by the abundant railroad bonds—by the mid-nineteenth century. Based on Henry Ford's comment, it would appear he held onto the Hibernia mine simply to hold out for a more lucrative market. The foundation of the Ford family's early wealth and prominence was no longer necessary by 1852. In fact, a potential purchaser of the land was very concerned about the less-than-optimistic outlook for the New Jersey iron industry. One hopeful purchaser commented in general the "mines must necessarily become much more valuable" in terms of future investment. This is partly a reason why Henry Ford was delaying to sell the land. The depressed nature of mining in New Jersey, and the depleted resources, made selling the land problematic.

Gabriel's Will

Gabriel Ford's will offers by far the most complete picture as to the extent of the Ford family's business ventures.[132] As the owner of the legacy property in Morristown (Gabriel bought out his brothers and sister in 1805), he can be seen as the penultimate owner of the most visible symbol of the family's rise to power in the American colonial period. The mansion—which Gabriel specifically mentions in his will—and the cherished two-hundred-acre tract of land on which it sits constitutes a direct line of descent that began when John Ford arrived in the colony of New Jersey in 1701. In 1848, nearly 150 years later, Gabriel Ford made out his will as a comfortable "country squire" and accomplished jurist.

Gabriel's will, dated January 27, 1848, was modern in terms of language and structure. Gone are all references to God and the thanks due him for the material prosperity of the testator. Gone are references to the transitory nature of life and the immutable laws by which we all must live. The language used by Gabriel was straight forward and economical—he did not waste words.

His wife, Frances, was mentioned first. "My beloved wife" is bequeathed "the use and possession of all my lands, tenements, hereditaments and real estate…during her natural life."

His son Henry Ford would be his principal heir. "All my lands, tenements, hereditaments and real estate…on the northerly side of the main road that leads from the public square in Morristown to my dwelling house, and thence directly

Historical marker with Fordville home in the background. The area around present-day Whippany was for a time known as Fordville and Monroe in the eighteenth and nineteenth centuries, when a grand-nephew of Jacob Ford Jr. built the home in the background. *NPS photo by Krystal Poelstra.*

Historical marker of Village of Monroe mentioned in Gabriel Ford's will. Between present-day Morristown and Whippany, Monroe was founded as a small community in the late eighteenth century before being enveloped into the town of Hanover. *NPS photo by Krystal Poelstra.*

to the village of Monore, I give...to my son Henry Augustus Ford...together with the mansion house, farm house, and all other edifices."[133]

To his grandchildren by his deceased daughter Anna Elizabeth, he leaves "all my lands tenements, hereditaments and real estate commonly called Cairo, situated lying and being near Mount Pleasant." This property amounted to over three hundred acres.

To his other children besides Henry (Edward, Lewis, Frances, Gabriel and Alfred) he left his remaining interest in "the mine at Hibernia." There are no other mine-related bequests made, and even this bequest of his portion of the mine was not absolute in terms of keeping an interest in the family. Gabriel instructs his son Henry to sell his father's portion of the mine for cash if it cannot be easily divided among his five children. Any other properties are to be divided among the six children "share and share alike."

United States Internal Revenue Tax on Legacies due to heirs of Gabriel H. Ford, nearly twenty years after his death. *Morristown National Historical Park.*

His wife, Frances, was mentioned once again in the final clause. She was to receive "the interest which…shall accrue on my bonds, notes and public stock, but without disturbing the principle of any of them." However, any executor was able to purchase more bonds, notes or public stock, with his wife's consent, to be added to his overall estate for her benefit and the benefit of his children.

HENRY A. FORD, THE LAST FORD (1793–1872)

In terms of the focus of this work, Henry A. Ford is the last of his line to own the Morristown mansion and the property that his grandfather Jacob Jr. had relied on to provide "an easy and comfortable life" nearly one hundred years earlier. After Henry Ford, the mansion—and the generations of Fords directly associated with it—entered history.[134]

Henry's Inventory

Henry A. Ford's inventory—taken at the time of his death—is interesting not only because it survives and offers a glimpse into the household belongings of someone who died over 130 years ago.[135] What makes Henry Ford's inventory unique is what he had in his possession in the mansion from the time Washington was there in 1779–1780. These items were still remembered and venerated as relics.

The inventory was conducted on August 31, 1872. The first floor hall was where mention is first made of memories of the mansion's past. Listed were two continental chairs and one Lafayette chair. Presumably these chairs were in the house and used during the continental period with one ostensibly used by Lafayette when he visited Washington in the spring of 1780. In the parlor, which was used as a conference room during Washington's stay, a Washington mahogany private secretary table was listed (visitors touring the mansion today can still see this).

In the northwest bedroom, a Washington chair was listed. The southwest bedroom, the master bedroom, was referred to as Washington's bedroom. Here was listed Washington's rush bottom rocker and Washington's looking glass. (A poem in homage to the mirror is found in Appendix B.)

Henry's Will

The first striking aspect of Henry Ford's will was its reversion to religious language and references. This is not surprising though given that Henry Ford was known as a very devout man. The second unusual aspect was that Henry states immediately that the will was "written with my own hand." Not unusual in the sense that he was a lawyer, but unusual in the sense that it was uncommon—most people did not write their own. Similarly, the religious language he uses had largely fallen out of favor in the nineteenth century as well.

Henry Ford makes mention in the first sentences to some of the challenges of his life,

> *Whereas since the making of a former will by me my beloved wife, Jane M. Ford departed this life and previous to her our lamented son Arthur Ford, who being a volunteer and taken prisoner with many other union soldiers, confined in Andersonville stockade prison in Georgia…*[and] *several of my other children having also departed without issue.*

The sad events recall a similarity to his grandmother Theodosia who endured terrible personal loss nearly one hundred years earlier in 1777.

The first bequest after the usual settling of debts was not to his family but rather to St. Peter's Church in Morristown (across the street from the Morristown Public Library today) where he had been a warden "almost ever since that church [had] been organized." The church was "of my love and choice," and with such strong feelings, he directed his executors to purchase "a lot of suitable size in the cemetery adjoining the church edifice." In addition, Henry Ford leaves to "our faithful and beloved rector, Rev. Robert Merritt, the sum of one hundred dollars." He also requests his children to care for his grave and that of their mother as well as those at the First Presbyterian Church of the earlier Fords.

Henry Ford's feelings toward his grandmother Theodosia, and a possible source of his piety, was evident in the following bequest (it will be remembered that Henry was the sole executor of his grandmother's not inconsiderable estate), "I wish my executors to divide among themselves and my other children my…family Bible, the large family Bible presented by my venerable grandmother, Theodosia Ford, to my honored father…containing family records, also an old Oxford edition of the Bible much prized and used by her containing like entries."

Henry mentions several other books by name including his Common Prayer book, the *Life and Writings of Bishop Duane*, Staunton's *Ecclesiastical Dictionary*, "presented to me by the learned and Rev. Doctor himself," Goodrich's *Pictorial Geography* and, finally, Irving's *Life of Washington*.

Henry Ford leaves his law library to his son-in-law, Frederic Ogden. Among further titles cited are Webster's *Dictionary*, Shakespeare's *Writings*, the *Works of Tacitus* and his father's copy of modern European history, which on the title page was Gabriel's "autographed signature and on its fly leaf a chronological key to English history showing the sovereigns from William the Conqueror to the reign of George the Third, inclusive." The list of book bequests was quite impressive. Henry Ford was obviously not just a well-read man; he wanted his family to follow his example in specific ways.

The family silver, stored in a bank vault in 1869, was to be divided among his family by a laboriously detailed distribution. Regardless of the minute detail of the bequests of the family silver, the overall dispersal was revealing of Henry Ford's commitment to his family and the larger ideal of family unity. This was a central concept running throughout all the bequests in the Ford family wills dating back to Henry Ford's great-great-grandfather John Ford's will in 1721. Henry also mentions furnishings from a "sick-room" that are not to be sold but maintained by the family. This was probably a reference to the final illness of his wife, Jane.

The most meaningful section of the will in terms of Ford family ownership of the mansion and surrounding grounds comes midway through the document. At the time he wrote his will, Henry Ford had the mansion under lease to his daughter Eliza and her husband until April 1870, at which time Henry presumably would move back into the mansion himself or perhaps lease it out again. There is a line that implies if he dies before the lease was due, they can stay until such time as it was due. His wishes concerning the mansion— or dwelling house, as he referred to it—are not in the least motivated by any sense of historical responsibility to the unique aspect of the mansion. Speculation could be nearly endless as to why, but according to his will, "it is my wish that my executors sell at public venue or otherwise dispose of it [at] their discretion" the Morristown mansion. A powerful reaction was generated from this simple statement.[136] His grandfather's house—his ancestors family homestead and a house made famous during the American founding—had seemingly met its end. Whatever the outcome, Henry Ford was resigned to let whatever would happen, happen, in terms of the sale of the family property. There was no indication that the family needed money, although Henry and his wife had a dozen children, of which although only seven lived to be adults.

It was Henry's wish that the proceeds from the sale of the mansion, grounds and personal items be divided between his surviving children. He wanted to divest the family of past holdings and provide for a new beginning perhaps for the next generation in the form of liquid assets. Henry's will represented an almost complete separation from the past.

No mention was made of iron, forges or furnaces. No outstanding obligations to anyone or due from anyone are mentioned. It is unknown whether Henry divested the family of iron interests intentionally or whether it was simply a matter of business. The iron industry did not hold anywhere near the prominence in 1870 in New Jersey as it did in 1770. And other Ford relatives were more involved in the business even though it was in decline, rather than the Morristown branch of the larger Ford clan by this time.

The End

Henry's will would seem to draw to a close the Ford family story in Morristown relating to the mansion. As a central figure to unify the family and provide for the family, the mansion and grounds had fulfilled their purpose. The mansion truly was a member of that family, not just a building. Without a main heir to continue the family business, which was no longer viable anyway, and without a family member to take over the estate, Henry did the inevitable.

Of course, his will was not the end. At the 1873 auction, conducted as per Henry's wishes (and one of the social events of the year), the mansion was purchased by four individuals with an idea to preserve the mansion as a historic site. In 1874, they formed the Washington Association of New Jersey and ran the mansion as a house museum before turning it over to the National Park Service in 1933 to be part of the first National Historical Park in the United States.[137]

SUMMARY OF FORD FAMILY WILLS

The Ford family wills—those of John Ford, Jacob Ford Sr., Hannah Ford, Jacob Ford Jr., Theodosia Ford, Gabriel Ford and Henry Ford—constitute the most personal aspect of their lives known to survive. Over the course of 150 years, several elements are apparent by their repetition. The connection to family is the most obvious. The line of descent that runs through the mansion in Morristown relied on their immediate and extended family over more than a century. In one respect, they resembled the landed planter aristocracy of the southern plantation in this devotion to, and reliance on, kin.

The most surprising will is Hannah Ford's, where she adjusts what she sees as the maladjusted will of her husband, Jacob Ford Sr. Hannah Ford was also the beneficiary of the largest single bequest of cash—£1,000. This enormous sum represented just one part of Jacob Ford Sr.'s estate and attests to the wealth the family had accumulated by the Revolutionary War. Another seemingly simple example is Jacob Ford Jr.'s request for mourning rings. While this request has a southern hint to it, the rings were not unknown in the north. In the south, they were exclusively for the wealthy members of society, and Ford Jr.'s request for several of the rings attests to his financial ability.

The wills of the last two generations to live in the mansion, those of Gabriel Ford and his son Henry Ford, indicate a basic approach to life. They are not extensive wills with great bequests or attempts to save humanity from itself through charitable contributions. Rather, both provide for their families first, just as their ancestors did. Theirs is a simple message of business, application and family. Their wealth was proprietary, not communal. They did not dissipate it on unworthy pastimes, and they did not keep assets beyond their useful period.

From a purely historical preservationist viewpoint, the most disturbing is Henry Ford's will with the provision to sell the mansion. By 1873, the mansion had become hopelessly out of date. Its size and style identified it as a relic of time gone by in a world focused on the future. Without the Washington connection, and the quickly approaching American centennial in 1876, Henry Ford's home may not have survived his death in 1872. The centennial in 1876 helped to raise consciousness concerning sites associated with America's founding, and this helped in the ultimate preservation of the Ford mansion. Historic preservation was not yet a concept recognized in the American approach to the past. Although Mount Vernon had been preserved in 1853, it was the exception. Naturally, it was not just the mansion's ties to the American founding. What made the mansion most attractive was the figure of George Washington. By 1873, Washington had been dead longer than he had lived. Yet once again he was being called upon in spirit to help heal the nation that was barely over the horror of the Civil War. His figure and memory ensured the survival of the mansion.

Aside from this desire of Henry Ford, his will indicates the family still had strong memories of certain family members. Particularly mentioned is Theodosia Ford, Henry's grandmother. Her ordeal must have formed the basis of many family stories about her strength that saw her and her family through 1777 and the decades following.

Part 3

The Family at Work

The Fords were involved with industrial commerce from virtually the very beginning of their time in the colonies. The Morris County line founder John Ford is believed to have started in the iron business in some capacity by 1715. The iron industry would be a part of the family's financial portfolio for over 150 years. This continuity could only be achieved through commitment and dedication to a guiding principle passed down through the generations. The final chapters in this work offer only an overview of the multiple business papers that exist to detail the family's involvement in the business world.

Chapter 4

Business Details

Methodology

As it would be extremely lengthy to document the business activities of just one Ford, let alone trying to condense all of them, the approach in this chapter will be to examine representative activities with the acknowledgement that much more information exists for further research. Naturally, more information exists for the later family members than for the earlier members, but the goal will be to represent each one in an effort to highlight the extensive network which the family built over a hundred years in business. As records describing John Ford are more difficult to come by, this overview will begin with his son, Jacob Ford Sr.

Land

Land was king in eighteenth-century New Jersey much like other commodities are today.[138] And as the Fords were an extremely active business family, it is not unusual to find the bulk of the surviving records relate to land transfers. One of the earliest documents recording a Ford Sr. business transaction is actually a copy of a circa-1738 document. The copy dates from about 1850 or 1860 and may have been a legal writing exercise for one of the younger members of the family at that time.

The copied document is a receipt from John Lindsley to Jacob Ford Sr. and the date of the original transaction was circa 1738. In the document,

Feb. 23 173 8/9.
[copied by Allen Ford ?] C 23

To All Christian People To Whom These
Presents Shall Come Greeting &c Know Ye
That I John Lindsly of ye Township of Hanover in ye
County of Hunterdon In ye Province of Newjersey &
Western Division of ye Same Yeoman for Divers good
Causes moving me thereunto but more especially
for and in Consideration of ye sum of Twenty pound
Current money of Newjersey to me in hand well
and truly paid before the Ensealing & delivery of these
present by Jacob fford of the same place aforesaid
Marchant the Receipt whereof I Do hereby acknowledge & my self to be therewith fully satisfied, contented
& paid & thereof & of every part & parcel thereof do
by these presents fully freely & absolutely acquit
Exonerate & discharge him the said Jacob fford his
heirs, Executors & administrators & every of them firmly
by these presents Have Given Granted. Bargained
Sold aliened Enfeoffed conveyd & confirmed & do
by these presents fully. freely & absolutely, Give
Grant bargain sell alien enfeoff convey & Confirm
unto him the said Jacob fford & to his heirs &
assigns forever all that one Certain tract or Parcel
of Land situate lying & being in the   of
Hanover. Beginning at a Post by Whippany River
Thence Running South forty five degrees East Sixty
Chains and Twenty five Links to a post for a

Copy of a 1738 transaction involving Joseph Lindsley and Jacob Ford Sr.
Original manuscript whereabouts is unknown. It was probably copied in
approximately 1850. *Morristown National Historical Park.*

Lindsley is identified as a yeoman while Ford Sr. is denoted a merchant. The document records a land sale from Lindsley to Ford starting "at a post by [the] Whippany River thence running south forty five degrees east sixty chains and twenty five links to a post...containing ninety acres of land." In terms of satisfaction that he has been adequately paid for the property, Lindsley states that he is "fully satisfied, contented, and paid and therefore... fully, freely, and absolutely...discharge[s]...the said Jacob Ford..." of any further obligation to him (Lindsley).

Ninety acres was a large parcel of land, and when combined with his other holdings, it simply contributed to Jacob Sr.'s standing as a major landowner in the area. Unfortunately, due to the crude survey standards of the time, it is nearly impossible to determine where some of the property lines were located. Even at the time, when a tree or stump or some other landmark was removed, accurately determining boundaries was a difficult business. This lack of precision and technology led to many court cases that today would not occur due to the technological advances in boundary surveys.

1,000 ACRES

In November 1764, Jacob Ford Sr. (given the use of "Esq." after his name) entered into an agreement to purchase 1,000 acres of land from the estate of Robert Hunter Morris, "late Chief Justice of the Province of New Jersey deceased."[139] Morris was the son of Governor Lewis Morris and "was in his lifetime and at the time of his death...[owner] of considerable real estate in the Province of New Jersey," and some of this land was being sold as per his last will and testament. Ford Sr. paid £1,000 or £1 per acre, for the tract. By the indenture between Ford Sr. and David Ogden and Richard Morris, they "do hereby acknowledge, and themselves to be fully satisfied, paid and contented [with] him the said Jacob Ford...[and] doth acquit exonerate and forever discharge" Jacob Ford from any financial obligation in terms of the purchase of the land. One thousand acres was a huge purchase of land. The £1,000 paid for it represents the same amount Ford Sr. later willed in cash to his wife, Hannah.

Purchasing from the illustrious Morris family was also probably part of the appeal of a purchase of this size. Dealing with the Morris family put Ford Sr. in contact with the very top of the American colonial social strata. While this may have offered some motivation for him, it probably was not the sole reason for making business decisions.

Purchase of one thousand acres of land by Jacob Ford Sr. from the estate of Robert Hunter Morris, 1764. *Morristown National Historical Park.*

ACTIVITIES OF JACOB FORD JR.

Land transfers were complicated transactions that required precise terminology and boundary description.[140] Among the scores of such legal manuscripts relating to the Fords are two from the mid 1760s.

In the first manuscript dated September 2, 1766, Jacob Jr. purchased from Thomas and Mercy Milledge about ten acres of land for "fourteen pounds proclamation money of New Jersey" and which the couple had purchased from the estate of Robert Hunter Morris, the same estate from which Ford Sr. had recently purchased 1,000 acres.[141] The Milledges may have been surveyors. In the agreement it states that "Thomas Milledge did survey in his own right" land that Ford Jr. was purchasing. The land in question begins "at a small white oak sapling marked on four sides with a blaze and three notches" on the eastern side. The tree is "standing north thirty five degrees west from the dwelling house…and north eighty two degrees east four

Thomas and Mercy Milledge's signatures on document pertaining to land purchase with Jacob Ford Jr. *Morristown National Historical Park.*

This Indenture made this Twenty Ninth Day of December 1766
Between John Salmon of the one Part of the Township of Roxbury
in the County of Morris and Province of New Jersey And Jacob Ford Jun.
Esq. High Sheriff of the County of Morris aforesaid of the other part
Witnesseth that We the s.d John Salmon for and in the Consideration of the Sum of Five Hundred pounds to him in hand
paid by him the s.d Jacob Ford Jun. Before the Ensealing &
Delivering of these presents, the Receipt Whereof he the s.d
John Salmon Doth hereby Acknowledge and himself to be
therewith fully and Entirely Satisfied Contented and paid
and thereof & of Every part and parcell thereof Doth
Homerate Acquit and Discharge him the said Jacob Ford Jun.
his Heirs &c. ad.ms and Every of them, by these presents
hath Given Granted Bargained Sold Released Conveyed &
Confirmed and by these presents Doth fully freely and
absolutely give Grant Bargain Sell Release
Convey and Confirm unto him the said Jacob Ford Jun. and
to his Heirs Ex.rs Adm.rs and assigns and to his and their only
Sole proper use Benefit and Behoof forever all one
Certain Tract or parcell of Land Scittuate Lying and
Being in the Townships of Roxbury County of Morris & Province
of New Jersey af.d Being all that Tract of Land which s.d John
Salmon purchased of Thomas Bowlby by Deed Bareing
Date the 2.nd Day of Novem.r 1758. Begining at an old Stooping
Chisnut Tree Standing in the Line of Thomas Whetherill and
Being the South Corner of the Land of George Bowlsby that He
Bought of His Brother Thom.s Bobby, And Runing from
thence along an old Line of Mark.t Trees of Thomas Whetherill
according to an old Survey South Eighty four Degrees West
Eighty Chains and Twenty & Six Links to a Large Chesnut Oak
Standing in the Line of the said Whetherill marked on four
Sides, from thence North fifty & Six Degrees East Twenty Eight
Chains more or less to another Corner of George Bowlsbys Land
Being a Small Black Oak, and from thence along said George
Bowlsby's Line Thirty four Chains more or Less to the

Indenture between John Salmon and Jacob Ford Jr., listing Ford Jr. as high sheriff of
Morris County, circa 1766. *Morristown National Historical Park.*

chains and thirty seven links from a mine pit called and known by the name of Smith's and Sniders mine." The land is described as possibly containing "mines, minerals, and ores" and was certainly purchased for that reason.

Shortly before the end of 1766, Ford Jr. entered into another purchase, this time with John Salmon. Dated December 29, 1766, Ford Jr., who is referred to as "High Sheriff of the County of Morris," bought 126 acres for £500. This property begins "at an old stooping chestnut tree" and was further identified by a "small black oak." What is interesting about this purchase were the circumstances around the deal and the caveat closing the sale.

John Salmon was sued by John Soward and lost the case. Salmon had been in the custody of the high sheriff (Ford Jr.) and apparently was released by Ford Jr.'s agreement to purchase 126 acres for £500. Whether Ford Jr. and Salmon knew each other or what exactly motivated Ford Jr. is not clear. Was Ford Jr. in the habit of buying "distressed properties" as it were, given his position as high sheriff? Probably not, and there is no doubt some reasonable explanation to complete the whole story; the surviving record does not indicate what though. The incident does show, however, how almost communal the approach to property sales could be at the time.

TWENTY POUNDS

Jacob Ford Jr. also lent money to private individuals as occurred in 1772. Samuel Crane of nearby Parsippany borrowed "twenty pounds, fourteen shillings, and three pence…together with the lawful interest." The bond was dated May 5, 1772, the same year that Ford Jr. started to build his mansion in Morristown. Even with this major building project, Ford Jr. kept up his business activities.

The bond is unique for another reason. References to dates are determined by reference to regnant years. The year 1772 therefore is denoted, "the twelfth year of the reign of our sovereign Lord George the Third by the Grace of God King of Great Britain, France, and Ireland." While completely common during the 1760s and earlier, it is somewhat unusual to see in a simple bond from 1772, especially when one party (Ford Jr.) soon became a well-known patriot.

By 1779, the bond was not repaid and Ford Jr.'s executors (remembering that Ford Jr. died in 1777) assigned the bond to Chilion Ford (a nephew). By 1779, the total due was twenty-three pounds, thirteen shillings and ten pence, which includes the interest due on June 1, 1779. The interest appears to have been paid regularly as the back side of the bond acts as a register of payments made and interest accrued.

HIS MAJESTY'S REGIMENT

As late as 1773—a year before the first Continental Congress met and when hostilities with England seemed more likely than not—Ford Jr. engaged with James Stevenson, Esq., "Captain in his majesty's sixteenth regiment of foot." The transaction involved £400 "current money of the Colony of New York" in exchange for a tract of land known as Long Meadow. Ford Jr., rather than purchasing, was in this instance "the grantor in the...deed

A 1773 business paper with Jacob Ford Jr. conducting business in New York on colonial stationary reflecting George III. Jacob Ford's signature is at the bottom. *Morristown National Historical Park.*

of conveyance" with Captain Stevenson. Although by this particular bond Ford Jr. was selling land, the bond references prior debts owed by Ford Jr. to Captain Stevenson, thus making for a complicated transaction.

The original transaction was dated August 5, 1773, and binds Ford Jr. to Captain Stevenson for £500 "current money of the Colony of New York." This clearly shows the Fords had intercolony interests and not just intracolony. Even as late as November 1775, after the outbreak of hostilities, Ford Jr. was paying interest due on loans to New York merchants. While the war created enemies, it did not always create a lessening of business. Twenty years later, after the passage of the Constitution, some of the earliest cases to reach the new Supreme Court involved British creditors and American debtors with disputes from the Revolutionary period.

The transaction with Captain Stevenson indicates the extensive and complicated nature of business dealings in the eighteenth century. While it is no different today, aside from the use of technology and the evolution of legal application to the types of affairs Ford Jr. engaged in, it still presented massive challenges and oftentimes could leave families destitute due to poor counsel and planning and overextension of obligations.

As it happened with the Ford family in 1777 after the deaths of Ford Sr. and Ford Jr., overextension of obligation became a real possibility. The type of extensive "empire" assembled by Ford Jr. needed constant attention. It also needed a knowledgeable administrator and the reputation established by her husband benefitted Mrs. Ford as she struggled to maintain the extensive financial relationships entered into by her husband and father-in-law.

Chapter 5

MRS. FORD AND
JOHN JACOB FAESCH

O f all the business activities that the Ford family engaged in over the years, some of the most dramatic occurred when the dominant Ford was a woman. Theodosia Ford, widow of Jacob Ford Jr., was left with an immense burden after her husband and father-in-law died within a week of each other in January 1777. Both men, planning to leave their estates to each other should one die, turned the family business on end by their ill-timed but incredibly coincidental deaths. While some aspects of the business ventures were sold off, such as the gunpowder mill to Joseph Lindsley, many other components remained to be managed and dealt with.

While her husband and father-in-law's reputation no doubt provided Mrs. Ford with a good starting point, the fact still remained that someone needed to take the lead and make decisions. That role fell disproportionately to Mrs. Ford, in conjunction with the executors.

Among the various activities that the Fords engaged in, the collaboration with John Jacob Faesch (the family's closest business associate) was one of the longest and most contentious of their ventures. After 1777, that venture became Mrs. Ford's to deal with. Faesch was renting the Mount Hope property where the Fords had extensive holdings and interests; the lease was initiated by Jacob Jr. in 1773, and was originally £400 per year. That amount was later reduced by Mrs. Ford to £220 per year as will be shown.

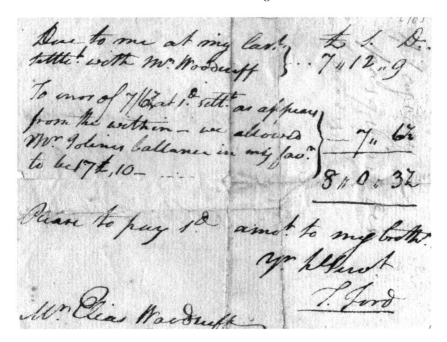

Account reconciliation by Theodosia Ford with her signature. *Morristown National Historical Park.*

TRANSACTING BUSINESS

Surveying existing records between Theodosia Ford and John Jacob Faesch show that, in some instances, payment on the lease by Faesch was not always made directly to Mrs. Ford in cash.[142] Rather than typical cash payments, Faesch would sometimes pay many of Mrs. Ford's expenses and the expenditures would be deducted from his lease obligation. In other words, if Faesch owed $100 (dollar amounts are purely for illustrative purposes) per month and paid $75 toward an expense of Mrs. Ford, Faesch would be left with a $25 payment remaining for the month.

In one account, which appears to date to 1782, Mrs. Ford's daughter Elizabeth took a shopping trip to Philadelphia. The list includes multiple entries for ribbons, satin, stockings, shoes, lace, stays and gloves. The colors indicated are not those associated with the perceived understanding of the Fords as dour Presbyterians. Colors mentioned include purple, blue, pink and red—all quite fashionable. The total bill came to £138, which Faesch records as "laid out for her daughter in Phil[adelphia]." Two years later, a similar payment occurred when Faesch paid money to

Mrs. Ford's son Gabriel who was a student at Princeton, ostensibly for tuition or living expenses.

In addition to the lease binding Faesch, he entered into bonds on at least two occasions with Ford Jr.'s estate and with Mrs. Ford directly. On December 24, 1781, Faesch entered into a bond with "Samuel Tuthill and Moses Tuttle, executors of Jacob Ford Jr., deceased." The amount of the bond was £2,145—in the currency of New York for the term of one year. Seven months later, on July 1, 1782, Faesch entered into a bond with Mrs. Ford for £1,000.

In another example, in August 1783, Theodosia Ford wrote a short note to record a transaction. The transaction itself is routine and somewhat meaningless except for the fact that it comes from Mrs. Ford's hand. The number of signatures—let alone notes or more extensive examples of her writing—is exceedingly rare. In the note, Mrs. Ford settles a small account and forwards a payment to her brother. Her signature, "T. Ford," is delicate and graceful and shows a glimpse of flowing artistry in penmanship.

With so much of the Ford family story missing, the seemingly minor or innocuous bits of information take on new meanings. Rather than incidental information, these small surviving items such as the signature become cherished for the slight light they cast on the Fords.

Business Issues

Theodosia Ford's management of her business interests is further displayed in a document from 1785. In the agreement, Mrs. Ford is clearly identified as acting on behalf of her late husband concerning the property at Mount Hope under lease to John Jacob Faesch. The term of the lease was twenty-one years, but by 1784, a problem had developed. According to Faesch, "the vein of ore on the premises from which he drew supplies for his furnace, hath become unexpectedly infested with springs of water, whereby it has become impracticable to tease ore…to his considerable damage, and the detriment of his works." In other words, Faesch could no longer afford the £400 rent.

The reduced business prospects meant reduced income. Aware of the situation, Mrs. Ford arranges for a reduction in rent. She "consented and agreed, and by these presents doth compromise" by allowing Faesch to lower the rent to £220 per year. However, Mrs. Ford leaves open the prospect of the mine returning to greater profitability. Should Faesch, "from the mine hole now open on the premises, or from any other vein or veins on the premises, and infested at present with water, or from the same vein of ore in any other place on the premises…raise and use ore of good quality, or as good as what was formerly raised from the large mine hole…as is fit and proper for the manufacturing of pigg or good refined bar iron…Faesch shall annually pay" the original £400 per year rent. Whether Ford Jr. would have been so accommodating under the circumstances had he lived is anyone's guess. The fact that Mrs. Ford was reasonable in this instance sheds some light on her as a person.

Chapter 6

A Difference of Opinion

Trying to Agree: Ford and Faesch

While we lack information concerning Mrs. Ford's personal life, we do have some material that highlights one area of her life in a way that sets her apart from most women of her time.[143] The business realm was predominately a male domain in the eighteenth and nineteenth centuries—and much of the twentieth too. With her husband and father-in-law so heavily involved in business activities, it was natural that perhaps she would find herself a part of those activities as well. The way she became a part was not what she anticipated though. After their deaths, she had little choice but to enter their world for the sake of her family. Surviving manuscripts show her involved not just in the years following her husband's death, but decades later when she was approaching her own death in 1824.

In 1784, some disagreement occurred between Mrs. Ford and John Jacob Faesch over the Mount Hope lease signed by Faesch and Ford Jr. in 1773 beyond the flooded mine issue referred to in the previous chapter. It has been discussed how Mrs. Ford agreed to lower the annual rent due because of flooded mines, which inhibited extraction of iron ore on Fresch's part. Whether a document from John Faesch titled "Answer to remarks and observations made by Mr. Timothy Ford…respecting Mount Hope Lease" is directly related to the flooding issue is not clear. Given that the two events occurred nearly simultaneously, it is hard to image the manuscript was not in some way prompted by the flooding event.

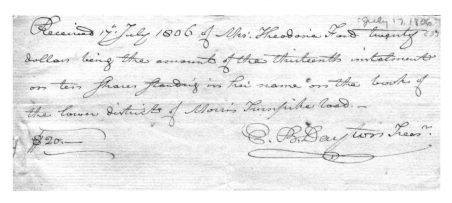

Receipts from 1808 for stock purchases in the Morris Turnpike Road for Theodosia Ford. *Morristown National Historical Park.*

The manuscript is over a dozen pages long and is dated December 4, 1784. The final agreement to lower the rent is dated 1785. Again, no direct link has surfaced, but it is more than likely the dozen-page missive from Faesch was part of the reason, in addition to the flooding, the rent was lowered.

Faesch was responding point by point in the manuscript to a report that Timothy Ford drew up concerning the Mount Hope lease and apparently heavily criticizing Faesch in it. It was his opinion—perhaps his mother, Theodosia, and the executors too—that Faesch was paying too little on his lease for what the Fords saw as valuable property that should return a greater profit on their investment. Timothy Ford's report tried to show the value of the land and the potential available—which Faesch was not meeting—and from this tried to justify the higher rent level.[144]

Faesch's response was interesting for its reference to the Revolutionary War and how that event should be taken into effect when determining how well Faesch had managed the property. Faesch saw that event as a major impediment to the maintaining of the business. Faesch also many times referred to the original lease drawn up by Jacob Ford Jr., whom he refers to as Colonel Ford. Overall, it is a remarkable document that testifies to the relationship the Ford and Faesch families had and how these relationships were often strained by forces outside of one or both parties' control. This was especially true concerning the Revolution. Many stories exist of how that event changed so many aspects of the political and social dimensions of peoples' lives. What is not always taken into account are the economic ramifications of the whole specter of the conflict. When viewed through the one scenario that occurred between Faesch and the Fords—and it is one of hundreds of similar incidences—the fuller impact, the longer reach of war is clearly seen. When businessmen like Faesch become victims without ever shouldering a weapon in anger, war can be defined as life altering. The customary patterns of interaction based on law and custom break down. In one sense, Timothy Ford and John Jacob Faesch are arguing about apples and oranges.

THE CASE SET FORTH

In essence, Faesch is arguing that his stewardship of the property has gone far and above what could be reasonably expected under the circumstances. The original rent was based on estimates arrived at by Jacob Ford Jr. "The supposed twelve hundred tons of ore in Colonel Ford's estimation" had not reached the value on the market that he anticipated and thus being half of the estimate it put Faesch at a serious financial disadvantage almost from the beginning. Furthermore, "the meadow has not yielded the one hundred tons of hay per annum, even the first two years, and has continued failing ever since." The pasture land is nearly worthless and "would not bear the expense of cultivating." The potential lumber "was of little or no note," and the pasture and woodland "cannot be looked upon as objects of value to the premises."

A section dealing with the large house built by Ford Jr. on the property is unique for its window on Ford Jr.'s approach to the property. According to Faesch, the house built at Mount Hope was discussed by Ford Jr. and Faesch before it was built as opposed to Faesch having moved into an already existing building as commonly accepted. As Faesch writes, "before any articles or agreements were executed, it was found necessary a dwelling should be erected." Faesch continues, "no request was ever made to Colonel Ford to go to a [great] expense" and that Ford Jr. was actually inclined to build a larger and more costly structure.

Faesch enumerates instances where he personally paid for repair and maintenance of the grounds that he claims went above what was expected of a tenant. The gristmill on the property—for which Timothy Ford thinks Faesch should pay a higher rent—was "built…mostly for his [Ford Jr.] own amusement, and to grind for his families use." The pond, blacksmith's shop, tools, stables and other items Faesch demonstrated he does not use and has no use for and therefore should not pay rent on them. He indicates these were all additions of Ford Jr. to the property. The iron ore reserves are certainly a major reason why the property was so valuable to both Ford Jr. and Faesch. For Faesch, iron ore was the main reason for leasing the site, "it was entirely from the prospect apparent [that] I built the furnace and came into an agreement to give so high a rent." And, as "the main object from which a profit was expected has entirely proved a disappointment," the rent should be adjusted accordingly.

Faesch further argues that "the heirs of Colonel Ford do not consider the many disadvantages I have labored under during the war"; "the difficulty of the times and scarcity of hands was such that I could not make more than one fifth part of the iron I should have made had it not been" for the war. Faesch taunts the Fords by proposing a hypothetical: suppose "I dropped the matter entirely and acted as my neighbors did [and abandoned the property], could the heirs of Colonel Ford in that case have expected rent"; "consider the risk I run in carrying on the works in the war, suppose the enemy had come up and burnt them totally, and destroyed my all, who would make me whole…?"

According to Faesch, Timothy Ford was completely out of line to attack Faesch as he did concerning the ironworks or other aspects of the property. The failure of Faesch's meadow—which Timothy Ford blames Faesch for—he claims was no different than others in the area. "Take a view of the neighboring meadows [owned and maintained by the Ford family]." So, why should Ford single out Faesch in his reasoning as a failed farmer if the family meadow is just as problematic? Faesch makes his case purely from the standpoint of an iron master, not a farmer, a blacksmith or any other trade. Faesch admonishes Ford that he never claimed talents he did not possess.

The issue of meadows was obviously a sore point for Faesch as he spent considerable space discussing the matter. He argues that some of the items Timothy Ford wishes to charge Faesch for, or to fault him with, are actually items that Jacob Ford Jr. was to have taken care of. In fact, according to Faesch, he already had better land for pasture himself than Ford Jr. was offering, so, "why then should I pay a rent for a piece of ground which in its primitive situation was not worth a farthing to me…?"

STRATEGY

Part of Faesch's plan in terms of his response was to show all the expenses he incurred for the land that he did not own. According to Faesch, he incurred property costs that were never anticipated when the original lease was executed. One particular sore point was "the very high taxes paid for the premises all [during] the war." Of similar interest and relating to cash, Timothy Ford apparently brought up the issue of the various types of currency in use at any given time and that Faesch should perhaps consider paying more because of the depreciated nature of some of the money he used in the recent past, which caused the Fords to lose some of the value of their rent paid by Faesch. To this, Faesch can only state that he used the same prevailing currency that everyone else used and can in no way be faulted for that. And, if Ford presses Faesch on this issue, Faesch can in turn charge Timothy Ford and the family, who used the same currency themselves, on exactly the same point.

In terms of the main purpose of the property—iron production—Faesch discusses two forges that he brought from the Ford Jr. estate. Ford Jr. had originally purchased the forges around 1775. Faesch acknowledges that Ford Jr. took a risk in investing at the start of a war. According to Faesch, Ford Jr. was the only investor found "[who] would risqué a purchase of iron works at so precarious a juncture, as the war was commencing and everything had a gloomy aspect."

Faesch concludes his lengthy response to Timothy Ford by cautioning him that regardless of what they determine between themselves, "unless the legislatures of the different states interfere, and stop importation of foreign iron, that it will become…out of the power of any Iron Master…to support and carry on" his business.

Finally, one of Faesch's most stinging criticisms aimed directly at Timothy Ford (who was only twenty-three at the time) was to compare his attack on him (Faesch) as something totally out of character with his father, the late Jacob Ford Jr.; "had Colonel Ford lived to have seen the difficulties arising from the disappointments…he would in that case have made all the allowances that in reason could be asked for." In other words, Timothy Ford—in Faesch's view—was not being reasonable and was not up to the business at hand as his late father would have been.

There is a genuine concern on Faesch's part to see an amicable solution to the problem. Whether what transpired between Faesch and Timothy Ford led to Mrs. Ford lowering the rent in 1785 is not fully clear, although from a circumstantial standpoint the episodes seem connected. The most important aspect of the situation between the families is that it shows how closely the Fords worked together as a team and how they relied on close relationships in business and socially. Finally, the episode also clearly shows Theodosia Ford as the manager and final decision maker in terms of the Mount Hope property. She is seen as actively engaged in the running of the family businesses.

Chapter 7

Canfield et al. v. Faesch et al.

FAMILY STRENGTH

The close relationship, professional and personal, between the Ford and Faesch families led to confrontation not just between the two families; they often found themselves as colitigants in larger cases where their combined business interests were concerned.

The death of John Jacob Faesch in 1799 set about a series of events that illustrates the connection between the Fords and John Jacob Faesch. Faesch, who died intestate, left an estate of considerable size and of sufficient attractiveness to generate lawsuits against it from anyone who felt a part of it belonged to them. Faesch unfortunately also left enormous debt that negatively counterbalanced his assets. Due to the interconnectedness of the two families' interests, the case resulting from his death—*Canfield v. Faesch*—ensnared the Fords in a long, costly, legal battle.[145]

By 1802, a bill of complaint had been lodged (by plaintiff Canfield), the defendants (Ford and Faesch) submitted their answer and the plaintiff had not responded. Gabriel Ford, who was acting as legal representative for the defendants, wrote to say that if a response from the plaintiff was not forthcoming that he would move to have the case dismissed. At this stage, Gabriel identifies Theodosia Ford (presumably due to her age) as one of the defendants against whom the case should be dropped; it was not. Theodosia Ford was in her early sixties and may not have cared to participate any longer as fully in the affairs relating to larger aspects of the families business holdings as in the past. Unfortunately for the Fords, the case continued.

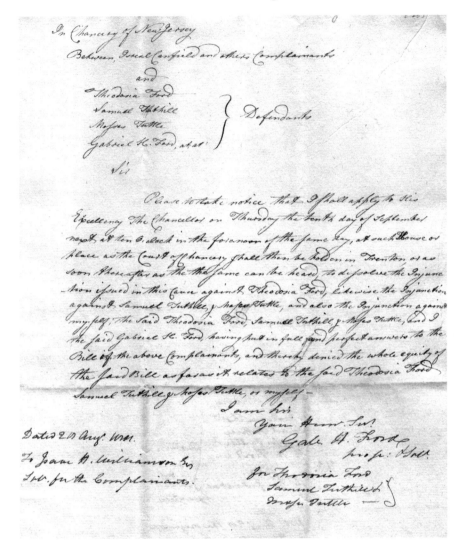

Letter of intent to ask for dismissal of Canfield suit by Gabriel Ford acting on behalf of defendants. *Morristown National Historical Park.*

According to statements of the several defendants, the Ford family entered into a partnership with John Jacob Faesch in a venture whose purpose was the "[selling of] merchandize, and of manufacturing iron at the said works." Faesch at this time possessed a "blast furnace…and teams, utensils and implements for carrying on" the business. Faesch also owned a "forge with four fires, a slitting mill and grist mill."

One aspect of the Canfield case (as the case will be referred to; Israel Canfield being the high sheriff of Morris County as well as a creditor of Faesch's and a plaintiff in the case against the Faesch estate) is the clear picture of Gabriel Ford as the head of the Morristown Fords. In the collection of papers, he is referred to as the solicitor and as the leader of the Ford family's business interests.

THE DETAILS

As per the defendants' response, the partnership they entered into with Faesch prior to his death enabled him to mortgage his holdings to pay some of his outstanding debt and to help fund his new business. As the company he formed progressed, Faesch would be allowed to recover his property as the prospects of the company improved. Records of all transactions were kept by the partners, and they indicated they had deposited the records in journal form with the clerk of the Court of Chancery.

According to the responses to the complaints against them in the defendants' transcript, "in the spring of seventeen hundred and ninety-six…John Jacob Faesch was largely and heavily indebted to the company at the time of its dissolution." The exact circumstances surrounding the dissolution of the business are unknown. The sum owed by Faesch was "exceeding six thousand nine hundred pounds" cash, but when combined with merchandize and stock at the company store bought on credit was factored in, the total was closer to "nine thousand six hundred pounds."

Faesch was clearly in debt. "Many of the creditors of the company were becoming impatient of the delay of payment and threatening to adopt coercive measures" when Faesch became ill with dropsy (edema). Faesch's imminent death caused consternation among his close business partners—later the defendants in the Canfield case—because they "would be expected as surviving partners to pay the debts themselves."

Shortly before his death, Faesch, after several visits from his investment partners, through a mortgage, offered "to take them [the debts] entirely upon himself in such a manner as to get these defendants exonerated." It is clear that Faesch had previously signed a contract with investors and was able to recover their investment for them. Within a week before he died, David Ford (a cousin of Gabriel), one of the investors and defendants, approached Faesch one final time, and "proposed to him to give these defendants a bond and mortgage, on his real estate, which…Faesch agreed to do." This was something Faesch wanted to do and had thought about. Additionally, it solved the problem of the immediate family investors but not of the other creditors hovering over Faesch. The purpose of Faesch's plan was "to indemnify and save harmless these defendants for the said Faesch's part of the debts still unpaid." Faesch mortgaged over eight thousand acres at Mount Hope to David Ford and others, ensuring they would receive payment before any other creditors. Of course this left them holding the land with multiple creditors arrayed against it.

In their answer to the plaintiffs, the defendants stated that Faesch "engaged to pay off and discharge the debts owing by the company and that he would relieve these defendants from the same." Faesch was adamant until his death that payment was forthcoming, "he often renewed his promises on this subject to the time of his death both to the defendants, and to the creditors in New York." Faesch was more than just talk however, as he "accordingly in the course of three years after the dissolution" made substantial payments to discharge the debt. Among payments Faesch received during this period from his customers was an undisclosed amount from the United States government. Whether this was a singular event, it shows Faesch and his colleagues with a wide and varied client base. It also shows that the government maintained business relations with Faesch and the area which was so important for iron production during the war.

The defendants seem to have taken advantage of their knowledge of Faesch's financial quandry and of his health in acquiring the bond and mortgage to secure their investment. The defendants state however in their deposition that they "deny all manner of unlawful combination and confederacy unjustly charged against them." The plaintiffs clearly thought something was happening behind the scenes with Faesch and the investors to protect their investment before anyone else's. Apparently, the creditors, separate from the investors, sought payment for several years. Unsubstantiated comments had some of the creditors already being made financially whole before Faesch died. These creditors disputed the "sundry persons, who were creditors of the company at the dissolution, deny having received payments of their demands from the intestate."

The defendants, including Theodosia Ford, stated "that the settlement was made free from all intention of fraud or collusion, with every equitable allowance in favor of the intestate." One of the creditors looking at the tangled mess of the Faesch estate was the United States government, to whom Faesch was a debtor and creditor.

In summary, Faesch was in business with the defendants. The plaintiffs were creditors of the company, and Faesch was essentially *the* company, while the defendants were investors. With Faesch's death imminent, the defendants sought to obtain what return on their investment that they could—they knowing the full story and Faesch's health. With the company and land turned over to the defendants, Faesch died intestate. Other creditors sued, but Faesch's company was no longer owned by Faesch; and the lawsuit began.

THE RESULT

The case ended with the court ordering Faesch's heirs to sell the estate with the proceeds going to the creditors, or the plaintiffs. The court also ordered that the costs of the suit to the defendants be paid from the sale of the estate.

On June 10, 1803, at the state house in Trenton, the Court of Chancery appointed John Doughty of Morristown a "commissioner and receiver" of the court. His job was to "sell and dispose of the land, tenements, hereditaments, and real estate in fee simple, late of John Jacob Faesch, deceased."

While the court ruled in favor of the plaintiffs, it found in part for the defendants by awarding them "cost-recovery" damages. The expense of litigating was to be reimbursed by the Faesch estate even though they technically lost the case. The legal reasoning aside, the Ford family came out quite well given that Gabriel Ford was their attorney and he would receive the payment as legal counsel.

WHAT THE CASE MEANT

In Canfield, the Fords are seen as determined business people. The Canfield case shows the interconnectedness of the family and how they protected their own by relying on familial strength to achieve a goal larger than just one person. The bonds forged through decades of business activity were clearly exhibited in this case. These types of connections were not uncommon; nonetheless, it is somewhat disturbing to read about how rough and tumble sometimes these partnership connections could make life for those involved.

Furthermore, it was even possible that Faesch purposefully died intestate. This would have enabled his family to utilize the property immediately and, in some cases, dispose of it before it came to the attention of creditors. In fact, the plaintiffs accused Faesch's heirs of precisely that tactic.

Lastly, the case rests on the fact that Faesch's heirs took control of the personal estate and claimed the worth was insufficient to pay the creditors. This, of course, cynically seems purely self-serving on their part. However, without more documentation, it is difficult to determine who was dealing with absolute truth. Perhaps neither side was actually. Both sides were competing for as much of a stake in the defunct business as possible.

Business relationships were notoriously difficult to manage given the primitive nature of banking during the period. Also, as already mentioned, the Revolution wreaked havoc with economic interests and many found it too difficult to adapt to the new banking regime under the new United States financial system. Perhaps someday more information on this case will be located and a fuller picture will emerge of the Fords as they rallied their forces in what was a major threat to their financial well being.

Chapter 8

Ford v. Tuttle

I n *Canfield v. Faesch*, the Ford family was drawn into a lawsuit through a business partnership. In *Ford v. Tuttle*, a similar reliance on business relationships was at the base of the case.[146] The difference with *Ford v. Tuttle* though was the involvement of family relationships through marriage. The case stemmed from the will of Jacob Ford Jr., who in 1809 had been dead for thirty-two years. Yet, it was that thirty-two-year-old will that formed the background for this case. It was also Ford Jr.'s wish and desire during what one of the defendants—his brother-in-law Moses Tuttle—called "those times of public confusion [the Revolution]" that formed the basis for the discussion of the case.

Moses Tuttle was married to Ford Jr.'s sister Jane, and Samuel Tuthill was married to Ford Jr.'s other sister Sarah; therefore they were naturally related. Both men were attorneys and both became active business partners when both Ford Sr. and Ford Jr. were alive. In his will, Ford Jr. made both men one of several executors. It is from this appointment that the *Ford v. Tuttle* case had its beginning. As executors, they were bound to carry out the provisions of the will. This included such unwritten clauses as ensuring the investments remain valuable and increase in value.

GABRIEL FORD'S COMPLAINT NARRATIVE

Of the executors named by Ford Jr., two proved to be ineffectual: his father, Ford Sr., died a week after his son died; and his father-in-law, the Reverend Timothy Johnes, "abstained as much as possible from secular cares."

The other two named executors, Moses Tuttle and Samuel Tuthill, were therefore left to handle the work themselves. As such, they had enormous responsibilities and power over the future of Ford Jr.'s children who would ultimately inherit his estate. After Ford Jr. died in January 1777, his father's death a week later threw the family into great disarray. Furthermore, in 1777, the Revolution was not progressing in the Americans' favor, and to compound issues, the economy was in shambles. It was during this period of family, social, political and economic turmoil that Tuttle and Tuthill took over as executors.

While it is unknown the exact role Mrs. Ford assumed in the weeks immediately following her husband and father-in-law's death, it is fair to guess that she was not much of a decision maker throughout 1777. Tuttle and Tuthill probably found Mrs. Ford too overcome by grief to participate in any meaningful way.

What Was Alleged

In the 1809 complaint filed by Gabriel Ford against Tuttle and Tuthill, they are accused of selling nearly two thousand acres of land at a cut-rate price to John Jacob Faesch. Not only did Faesch allegedly receive a bargain, he paid in depreciated continental currency; on top of that, Moses Tuttle is accused of losing what little value the currency had in a poor investment.

> *Although the infatuation of converting real estate at so late a period into perishing continental money was ever lamented by the children of the testator, they patiently submitted to it as an error of judgment in which the trustees had no conceivable benefit to themselves and rose above all suspicion.*

According to Gabriel, while the children may have accepted the loss with no malice attributed to their uncles, they "never requested an account or settlement of their father's real or personal estate, nor have those accounts ever been rendered or settled by the said executor's or trustees to this time." In fact, "no reason for questioning the truth and uprightness of the…sale had been known for 30 years till about the 28th day of December" 1808 when a new survey was conducted for a neighboring property. From this survey, it was discovered that, in fact, Moses Tuttle had not sold the land to Faesch but rather kept it as his own and even filed a deed to that effect, which ultimately was discovered by Gabriel Ford, thus igniting the lawsuit.

According to Gabriel, he found this "astonishing and almost incredible until Moses Tuttle's own acknowledgement." Samuel Tuthill, on the other hand, denied all knowledge, and Gabriel Ford found "the disclaimer perfectly sincere and conscientious."

Therefore, Gabriel Ford alleges that "all the formalities of the pretended purchase and a [series] of fraudulent devices to conceal the real truth of a secret agreement that was made" between Faesch and Tuttle. The whole plot thus having been conceived by Faesch and Tuttle, allowed them to use the cover of a bad deal, the disruption of the war and the deaths in the family to cover up any untidy questions. Tuttle was believed to have easily obtained the concurring signature from the two other executors—Timothy Johnes and Samuel Tuthill. The Reverend Johnes was portrayed as not wanting to be bothered and simply agreeing to sign without knowing; and Tuthill being too ill to take notice at the time.

Gabriel Ford sums up his complaint:

> *The sale to John J. Faesch…was a real bona fide transaction, and all the money was to have been collected accordingly, but that John J. Faesch proving unable to pay the whole he, the said Moses Tuttle took back the 996 acres on that account thereby admitting that John J. Faesch has never yet paid for that part of the premises; and your Orator* [Gabriel Ford] *humbly ventures that if a part of the premises were taken back for default of payment, it should have been taken back in the names of all the trustees and not of one alone in a secret deed.*

Even though Moses Tuttle was his uncle, and the families had been close for decades, Gabriel charges Tuttle "insidiously pushed forward [his plan]…for the secret purpose of converting" the land to his own use. Tuttle is accused of selling wood and iron products too from Ford land as his own. Gabriel asks the court to order Moses Tuttle to "Convey to your orator so much as remains unsold of the said 996 acres, and to pay to your orator a fair price for such as has been sold."

THE DEFENDANT'S SIDE: "EXTRAVAGANT FICTIONS"

As might be expected, Moses Tuttle starts by offering a swift defense of his actions and by providing a brief review of the events of 1777 in the Ford household. Tuttle reminds Gabriel Ford that he was only a child at the time and could not fully comprehend the magnitude of the loss suffered by Theodosia Ford and the larger family.

Contrary to Gabriel's assertions in his complaint, the Reverend Timothy Johnes, father of Theodosia, was far from disengaged with events in 1777. According to Tuttle, the Reverend Johnes was "so nearly connected with the children…in their state of domestic affliction…[and did] take a constant and close interest in all that concerned their property and welfare." Tuttle claims not to know what has come over Gabriel Ford; but he "seems to have given up himself to unreasonable suspicions and indeed extravagant fictions" in the narrative of his answer to Gabriel's complaint.

Moses Tuttle references the property at Mount Hope as described by Gabriel as "comprehending two forges out buildings and houses in complete repair, a most valuable mine and nineteen hundred and forty five acres of woodland in an excellent situation" as being with "great incorrectness." Tuttle does however allude to the work going on at the site in support of the Revolution, the ironworks having "contracts with Congress for furnishing large supplies of cannon balls, shot and other munitions for the United States and during the whole or nearly whole of the Revolution." According to Tuttle, the allegations put forth by Gabriel Ford that he and Faesch "colluded together to defraud his widow and infant children…are not only improbable but absolutely groundless and untrue" and are uniquely unworthy of coming from the defendant's nephew.

Defending himself further, Tuttle states:

> *This defendant was the brother in law and friend of Col. Ford and appointed by him executor of his estate and bound by an obligation of justice and relationship to perform his will and execute the trusts thereof faithfully—is it conceivable that within a few months after his death and indeed in almost the very first transaction of the estate that this defendant entered into a combination so cruel and detestable with Mr. Faesch…?*

Moses Tuttle relies on his service or "the prosecution of honest industry in the cause of his country in the militia" to validate his character.

Vignettes

Throughout Tuttle's narrative there are glimpses of the wealth and power of the Ford family at the time of Ford Sr. and Ford Jr.'s death. There are also hints of Tuttle's relationship with the family and hints at how the family operated and relied on close associates. Speculating and reasoning to the fact that he (Tuttle) would not have a desire to defraud the family, he points out that as son-in-law to Ford Sr., he would have been in line, through his wife, of inheriting a "great estate." While it is not known what Tuttle meant specifically by great estate, the manner in which he uses it signifies that it would have been substantial enough to remove any malicious tendencies toward the rest of the estate.

In another instance, Tuttle refers to "a large tract of about 4000 acres bought by Col. Ford himself about the year 1774 of the proprietors." Four thousand acres was an enormous tract of land, and its sole purpose was industrial investment. This amount alone made the Fords one of the largest landowners in the area. But when combined with their already existing properties, it put them in the highest levels of business power in the county. Also, as has been mentioned, the fact that Ford Jr. was still making deals as late as 1774, the year of the First Continental Congress, is significant in itself. The man who would die serving his country, and be known for that more than his business achievements, was evidently not overly reticent about taking on debt in the midst of a political calamity.

Moses Tuttle Continues

While admitting the sale through the deeds Gabriel Ford cites in his narrative, he does so "solemnly denying however that either of the said deeds are fraudulent or that the property was sold by the executors or procured to be sold by the defendant as one of them below its then obtainable value." In this nutshell was Tuttle's whole defense: Gabriel Ford acknowledges the sale occurred as Tuttle claims, however, the *process* of the sale alleged by Gabriel Ford is not accurate, according to Tuttle.

In a moment of frustration, Tuttle maintains that after thirty years "it might be placed beyond the power of this defendant to do more than trust to his character and oath and to the fair reputation of Mr. Faesch." He has no doubt, even if his memory is fading, that he was convinced of his "innocence and indeed he cannot but hope [that he] would remove from the mind of his nephew the complainant his unreasonable and ill founded suspicions." This comes up multiple times throughout the narrative; the defendant "at so great a distance of time has been unable to recollect and prove the particular circumstances under which the deed…was made." Tuttle continues: "complainant ought not to be permitted after thirty years from a transaction of this nature to be allowed to impeach it, or claim any benefit or estate therefrom."

The entire episode initiated by Gabriel Ford brought nothing but ill repute on Tuttle in his advanced years after a life of integrity and studious application:

> *This defendant may surely be allowed to express his just surprise as also to state the injury done to him by such manifest misrepresentations by the complainant made with a view to draw down suspicion upon his conduct and to impress a belief of his having acquired fortune and riches by defrauding the widow and children of his deceased friend and relation when in truth and in fact his study and care have been exerted for their happiness and propriety.*

In fact, Tuttle states that "this defendant was obliged to furnish and advance money of his own to the widow of said Jacob Ford Jr. for her own subsistence and that of her children."

It is difficult to know the relationship that existed between Tuttle and Gabriel Ford in 1809. Theodosia Ford, the "widow Ford" referred to by Tuttle, was still alive and must have had some viewpoint on this matter. Similarly, given that her father, the Reverend Johnes, was so intimately involved in the whole affair by the simple fact of being her father and the grandfather of her children, it would be strange that she would not have had a part in the suit. Also, Mrs. Ford's own troubled business relationship with John Jacob Faesch would have made her probably inclined to be apprehensive of the Tuttle defense, even though Tuttle himself was less than encouraging about some of Faesch's business practices, regardless of what he was like personally.

Tuttle exposes another interesting point in relation to Ford Sr. and Ford Jr. and the way their business relationship functioned. According to Tuttle, Ford Jr. died with large debts and little in the way of liquid assets; whereas Ford Sr. had few debts and high liquidity. This would indicate that the son had taken on many of the business ventures while the father withdrew from active engagement.

The debts referred to for Ford Jr. were business in nature rather than personal. The debts in themselves also provide evidence that, contrary to pulling back from the business world during the war, Ford Jr. was actively engaged and no doubt saw his best option as that of breaking with Britain. That, of course, raises its own questions as to how much his resistance to Britain was motivated by investments and the expectation of losing them. While it is difficult to prove one way or another without some type of "smoking gun" documentation, historical theorists have long suspected that some patriots were driven more by their concern over their investments than by burning desires for something more ethereal like freedom or liberty. Money and the material consequences of having it were—and still are—tangible. One does not have to try and define success when it can be displayed.

The war though—whatever the motivation—was never far from anyone's memory. And Tuttle reminds the court that "when the times are considered viz 1778 and 1779 and how many impediments and irregularities were produced by them this honorable court will rather be surprised at so much formality as took place in regard to these deeds." In other words, Tuttle is reminding those who were quite young during the war that normal business practices were not always followed. Indeed, it is a wonder they accomplished what they did given the difficulties they faced.

It will be recalled that in John Jacob Faesch's dispute with Timothy Ford and Theodosia Ford over rent payment, Faesch too factors into his argument that the war brought undue burdens on his business prospects. Yet, nowhere does either of these men employ patriotic language to justify what occurred. It was simply the exigencies of the times, which, as with Ford Jr., begs the question as to why they and many others chose the route they did during the conflict with Britain.

From Tuttle's view, the assertion that the knowledge of the ownership of the property has been anything but a secret is firmly established. In fact, Tuttle asserts that he had been publically paying tax on the land for decades—hardly something one can do secretly. He also publically sold portions of the land and had openly worked the land for decades.

Tuttle wishes that "the complainant, his nephew, [to] calmly review this subject and give but a reasonable credit to this defendants age, character and oath, his relation to the family, and the circumstances now made known." Not only is Tuttle in 1809 "impaired with age," but the "shock given to his mind and heart by an imputation so disgraceful and untrue" that his reason is almost overcome. The hurt Tuttle feels is palpable in his narrative, and as he continues, he becomes more inclined to attack Gabriel. He uses terms like "imbecile," "ignorant" and "child" to describe the various attitudes taken by Gabriel Ford in his accusations. Tuttle remonstrated Gabriel that his behavior "in this defendants opinion [is] no way becoming that respect which was due between strangers, much [less] from a nephew to an uncle."

THE RESULT

Gabriel Ford was unmoved by the answer provided by his uncle Moses Tuttle. Gabriel writes that the "defendants [narrative] is uncertain, untrue, and insufficient" as to the particulars of his (Gabriel) charges.

Unfortunately, among papers pertaining to this case, there is not one indicating the outcome. However, from the papers that do survive, it is clear that the evidence against Moses Tuttle was building. Numerous entries cite the inconsistent stories as to the events and more witnesses seem to concur with Gabriel Ford's version of events.

Regardless of which party won at court, neither party really "won" anything. The damaged reputations, the ill feelings and the sense of betrayal meant a loss of human proportions for both Gabriel Ford and Moses Tuttle. Gabriel Ford probably had the more difficult task in defending what he saw as his family's honor and well being. The sacrifices endured by his mother during the war were made only more bearable when Gabriel felt her sense of pain in her place through her memory by the actions of Tuttle that were unfolding before Gabriel's eyes. To the extent the record exists, Gabriel tenaciously pursued his family's rights as he saw them. Gabriel undoubtedly witnessed the quality of devotion to family in his mother during the difficult years following Jacob Ford Jr.'s death.

All in all, it is a sad way to end a story, but it is indicative of the difficulties faced by families like the Fords. Their story was sadly not unique. The same scenarios which produced the situations presented above played out in similar fashion throughout the country.

Conclusion

Who then, were the Fords? While their beginnings are not as clear as we would like, it is certain that by the mid-eighteenth century they had established themselves as one of the most prominent families in the county. While this was primarily through the efforts of Jacob Ford Sr., his reliance on his son Jacob Ford Jr. and an extended family network through marriage moved his influence beyond his singular person. This enabled the Fords to prosper and to keep the family business close to the hearth.

This closeness though also created multiple opportunities for tensions to escalate. In an era of extensive litigation, the Fords minimized this costly endeavor by keeping so much of their work among themselves. However, this did not always work. The general path of businessmen during this time was extensive legal activity, mainly relating to the purchase and sale of land. Real estate was valuable in and of itself, but with the added feature of iron ore resources, the land became even more valuable and thus more covetous. As the Canfield and Tuttle cases show, family ties only insulated their business activities to a certain point. When necessary, the courts were employed.

The larger significance of the Fords is their reflection of the events unfolding around them. Rather than be helplessly attached to tradition, they reasonably moved on as circumstances dictated. Their triumphs and defeats are emblematic of the developing societal patterns taking shape in the United States.

One of the more succinct examples of the dramatic changes facing America's prominent Revolutionary families was the story of the Tucker

Calculations of payments with interest due to Jacob Ford Jr. and his heirs by 1777.
Morristown National Historical Park.

family of Williamsburg, Virginia. A study of their rise and fall is symptomatic of many of the challenges facing the generations who brought about Revolution and the generation who immediately became the inheritors of that event.

The parallels are certainly not exact between the Fords and the Tuckers (and there is no evidence they knew of each other). The contrast does however serve to highlight the differences that existed during the period of American national development. Whereas the prominent Tuckers failed to keep pace with the evolving socioeconomic patterns developing in the young republic, the Fords on the other hand seemingly embraced the burgeoning market forces empowering the new nation. While the geographical dissimilarities no doubt contributed to the approaches each family had toward life, something else was clearly at work.

It is known that the Tucker family patriarch, St. George Tucker, strongly encouraged his family—including his famous stepson John Randolph—to move beyond the planter-based, slave-dominated social and economic patterns that dominated tidewater Virginia. His children, however, held on to the old traditional ways of delineating their lives. This greatly distressed their father, who saw the failure of the pre-Revolutionary-era economic lifestyle and urged his descendants to move to a more sustainable industrial pattern and approach to life. St. George Tucker was a man ahead of his time that saw the Revolution as more than just a victory over the British. Tucker saw that the entrenched ways of economic life that predated the war could not be sustained after independence was achieved.

The Fords, on the other hand, clearly embraced the new world formed by the Revolution. Although we don't know if Mrs. Ford advised her children the way St. George Tucker did his, it is certain they received guidance from someone. Whatever the impetus, we do know that the Fords moved to eliminate the problems associated with the declining iron business in New Jersey through other investments. They embraced the new technologies through investment. The last Ford to live in and own the mansion, Henry, had obvious fond memories of his grandmother, Theodosia Ford, and her generation that fought the Revolution—but this did not restrain him. Their outlook was the future, not the past, even to the point of selling their cherished mansion or some of the long-held iron mines.

While the Ford family passed from the historical record after 1873, their story did not. While a product of their time, the Fords were not confined to their time by refusing to acknowledge that time moves on. They did not dwell on past-perceived wrongs longer than necessary and dealt with adversity as it came. Theirs was a family story, a New Jersey story and, finally, an American story. The common thread linking them all was the human story. They cared for family and treasure through some of the most transformative times in history, and this work is no doubt not the last word of their tale.

POSTSCRIPT

The Fords of Morris County, New Jersey, were not the superheroes of the eighteenth century. Their names would probably be lost except for the fact that George Washington spent six months in their mansion in 1779–1780. Without that one event, much of what little has been preserved about them would probably not have been, including the mansion. Even with what we have today of their manuscript remains, we are still forced to piece together a story of their lives much at times to the detriment of historical accuracy. Basing a story on supposition can be a tricky business and should only be attempted with caution. That is why encouraging further research is so important. Someone else may find another bit of information, and someone else something more, and so forth. At the beginning of this work, it was stated that it is hoped that this study will encourage others to take up the story of the Fords, not just for the sake of research itself, but rather to continue to fill in the often sketchy outlines we have of eighteenth-century New Jersey.

Much has been made over the years about how New Jersey's history is overlooked and unappreciated. That is partly because the same story New Jersey tries to tell is told in hundreds of other places outside of the state. For New Jersey history to be uniquely New Jersey, it needs to be about New Jersey and what New Jerseyans did—not what others who encamped in the colony or state did and then left. Local history and local understanding of what we were and are come predominately from internal sources. External sources are simply flavorings to the story, not the story themselves.

As such, the Fords represent one family and one portion of the overall macro story that is New Jersey history. The amount of material lying in archives around the state that chronicle the events and people of this area is breathtaking. A student looking for a topic would not have to go far to find not just information, but primary source information available to them for a report, thesis or even dissertation.

Appendix A

IRON INDUSTRY IN MORRIS COUNTY

This appendix was developed from the companion booklet to an exhibit on Morris County iron curated by the Morris County Historical Society. The exhibit ran from November 2003 to March 2004 and was titled "Forging the Future: The Iron Industry of Morris County."

ACT OF BRITISH PARLIAMENT

In 1750, an act of British Parliament was passed that threatened Morris County's fledgling iron industry. The act prohibited the building of rolling mills, slitting mills, plating forges or furnaces. Those industries that already existed were required to report the full details of their establishments to the sheriff. This legislation was an attempt to prevent the colonies from making their own iron products and to ensure that the iron supply would go directly to Great Britain for production. Like so many of the eighteenth-century acts passed by Parliament to ensure the American colonies dependence on the mother country, it was by and large ignored.

David Ogden built a covert slitting mill in Boonton. The slitting mill was on the lower level of a structure used as a gristmill, so that the slitting mill operation could be disguised when necessary. Ogden allegedly put his gristmill ruse to good use when Governor William Franklin arrived for an inspection. Upon Franklin's arrival, Ogden invited him to have dinner at his home. After a hearty meal and numerous drinks, Franklin made the inspection and found nothing illegal about the operation. There has been speculation that Franklin himself was an investor and was eager to turn a blind eye. Nonetheless, the story has become part of the early lore and history of Morris County's iron industry.

CREATING IRON FROM ORE

Furnace

In order to remove iron from iron ore, it was necessary to heat the ore with a charcoal fire. Due to its carbonaceous nature, charcoal when heated draws oxygen, therefore removing oxygen from iron ore and leaving behind a more pure form of iron. The early iron furnace was a twenty-foot, four-sided structure built of stone or brick on a hillside. The furnace was tapered toward the top. Inside the building was a lining of sand or broken stone, which insulated the inner core of firebricks. At the bottom was the crucible that received the molten iron. Above the crucible were openings for the air-blast nozzles, called tuyeres. The air blast was created by a giant water-powered bellows, which was set up next to the furnace.

A combination of iron ore, charcoal and limestone, called a "charge," was fed into the top of the furnace. A hearth was then heated at the bottom of the furnace structure. At the top of the furnace chamber, a chemical reaction occurred that turned the iron ore into metallic iron. The metallic iron had a lower melting point than the rest of the mixture, so the liquid iron collected at the bottom of the furnace and the remaining material or slag floated to the top. As the iron separated from the ore, the molten iron would be drawn off through an outlet in the furnace. It was run into sand channels that led the molten ore to the casting house where molds created the "pig" iron.

Iron Ore

Morris County iron ore was generally a magnetite ore. It could be shipped out or sent to the crusher where it would be broken down into even smaller pieces. Iron ore that had low iron content would be pulverized into powder and then separated, creating iron powder.

Finery and Chafery

The furnace was the first step in creating iron from iron ore. After the pigs were cooled, they were taken to the finery or forge. Here the iron was partially melted by a charcoal fire and again blasted with air. The air blast removed carbon from the pig iron by converting it into carbon monoxide and carbon dioxide. The iron became purer and coagulated into a spongy mass called a "half bloom." The half bloom was hammered under a large hammer, also water powered, to further remove impurities. The final step was to again heat the bloom in another charcoal furnace called the chafery. Here the bloom was forged down into a finished bar of wrought iron.

Related Operations

A full-scale iron works that converted iron ore into wrought iron and finished products included a furnace, finery and chafery. Each of these operations was housed in different buildings and each had their own fires. These were not the only buildings and operations needed to process iron, however. Men were employed to cut down wood from local forests. The wood was then transported to a charcoal house. In many cases there was no formal structure for burning wood and creating charcoal. The wood was simply stacked in cone-shaped bundles, covered with damp leaves and ignited. Either in the charcoal house or in the bundle, the wood was slowly burned until it became charcoal. In yet another building, a carpenter or carpenters were employed. The carpenters created the wooden patterns for iron products. In casting or molding houses, these wooden patterns were used to create the sand casts that molten iron was poured into to create a finished product.

MORRIS COUNTY IRON AND THE REVOLUTIONARY WAR

The presence of the burgeoning iron industry in the Morris County area certainly played a factor in General George Washington's presence in the area; however, it was not the primary motivating factor it might seem. The availability of iron ore and the various workings to fashion it into objects represented a valuable resource to the Continental army. Evidence indicates that shot and other materials for the Revolutionary cause were made at local sites. Letters written to Colonel Henry Knox, chief of artillery under Washington, from Joseph and Charles Hoff, who were operating the Hibernia Furnace, indicate their willingness to provide shot, cast cannon and to provide other supplies the army might need. Unfortunately, the rich iron resources of the area never developed into a major supplier during the Revolutionary War. Lack of supplies and manpower, which hampered the army, also hampered the iron industry.

John Jacob Faesch (1729–1799)

John Jacob Faesch was born in Basel, Switzerland, in 1729 and came to America in 1764. Faesch worked as the manager of an iron factory in Germany and was offered a seven-year contract to manage the ironworks of the London Company (also known as the American Iron Company) in Ringwood, Charlotteburg and Long Pond, New Jersey. Peter Hasenclever, the general manager and superintendent of the London Company, arranged for Faesch, his wife, and his servants' passage to America. He was to be paid 2,500 guilders a year, given a suitable home and land to live on and the option to engage in other business, as long as it did not interfere with the company's interests.

Unfortunately, Faesch's wife died en route to America, so he began his new life in America alone. As manager, Faesch successfully ran all of the mines, forges and ironworks in the area for the London Company. By introducing his knowledge of modern iron manufacturing techniques, he was able to improve the output of iron products in Morris County.

In 1770, Colonel Jacob Ford Jr. offered the sale of his manor house, gristmill, flax mill, two other houses and assorted outbuildings in the Mount Hope section of Rockaway to Faesch. With his seven-year contract with the London Company about to expire, Faesch leased the land from Ford in partnership with Daniel Wriesburg and began cultivating the richest iron mines in the county.

A year later in 1771 when Wriesburg died, Faesch inherited his estates. With the money he purchased more land for his "Great Mount Hope Tract," where he built a large furnace in 1772. Eventually he owned over six thousand acres of iron-rich property in Mount Hope. This did not include the many other forges he owned, operated or leased in the county, making him the leading ironmaster in the state.

During the Revolution, his iron mill played a crucial role in producing munitions for the Continental army such as shot, shell and cannon. During the war, he owned outright, or with partners Hibernia Furnace, the Brookland, Mount Pleasant and Longwood Forges.

Faesch leased the Hibernia Ironworks from Lord Stirling from 1780 to 1781. They were managed by Charles Hoff Jr. In 1781, he became associated with the Boonton Ironworks by leasing a 2,500-acre tract, a forge, splitting mill and gristmill. The ore came from his Mount Hope Furnace.

Faesch was well-known in the county as a prominent ironmaster and political voice. He was an ardent Whig, a justice of the peace and a county judge. Faesch was a member of the convention organized to ratify the new American Constitution and established New Jersey as a state in 1787. He married Elizabeth Brinckerhoff in 1775 and Susan Lawrence in 1790.

John Jacob Faesch remained the sole operator of the Mount Hope mines when he died in Boonton in 1799. He also owned the Mount Hope manor house, Middle Forge, Boonton Forge, Jackson's Forge, a share in the Morris Academy and several lots. His two sons, John Jacob and Robert, took over the operation of the mines, but they did not prosper. The Boonton Ironworks under his son Robert B. Faesch operated until 1820 when he became insolvent. John Jacob Faesch is buried in the cemetery of the Morristown Presbyterian Church on the Green.

THE FORD–FAESCH HOUSE

The Ford–Faesch House is located in Mount Hope in Rockaway Township, New Jersey. It was built on lands originally acquired in the middle part of the eighteenth century by Jacob Ford Sr., a wealthy entrepreneur who was influential in Morris County's iron industry. He bought the property in order to take advantage of the area's rich iron deposits. In 1768, Ford conveyed the Mount Hope property to his son, Colonel Jacob Ford Jr.

Colonel Ford proceeded to build a spacious Georgian manor house on the land. The two-and-a-half story house was constructed on a promontory overlooking the valley. It was made of native stone and had walls that were three feet thick and symmetrical wings on the east and west sides. There were twelve large rooms, nine English-style fireplaces and a smokehouse in the attic. Its total cost was approximately £1,400.

In 1772, Colonel Ford leased the house and its associated ironworks to John Jacob Faesch. Faesch and his family lived in the house as if they were aristocracy, employing several servants and using a private carriage with uniformed footmen. During the Revolutionary War, George Washington often visited the Ford–Faesch House. On one of his visits, he gave Faesch permission to employ thirty-five Hessian prisoners of war in his mine.

Faesch lived in the manor house until the 1780s when he moved to Morristown. After he left, the mansion was continually inhabited by the owners, superintendents, engineers and department heads of the Mount Hope Mining Company. In the last quarter of the nineteenth century, a Victorian front porch, fancy eave ornaments and bay windows were added to the house, while the west wing was removed.

The house lost its upper class status in the 1920s when it was used as a boardinghouse for mine workers. In 1931, the manor house was converted internally into a two-family dwelling and electricity was added. It became a single family home again in 1955 and was so occupied until 1973 when the Halecrest Corporation, which owned the mining operation at the time, went bankrupt.

Due to its continual mining company ownership, the Ford–Faesch House has been able to preserve much of its original colonial materials. Renovations had been made by covering up earlier material rather than removing it as would have been done by a private owner. As a result, the colonial material has been protected over the years under later period fabric.

The Ford–Faesch House was placed on the New Jersey Register of Historic Places in 1973 and the National Register of Historic Places in 1974. Rockaway Township acquired the house and two acres of surrounding land in 1982 for $35,000. The township leases the property to the historical society of the Rockaways, whose members have assumed responsibility for safeguarding and restoring the house.

Mount Hope: 290 Years of Industrial Tradition

Early Development

Early settlers began mining iron ore at Mount Hope around 1710; except for brief periods, the mines have been worked almost continuously for over 290 years. After the iron mines closed in 1959—and again after their brief reopening in 1977—operations at Mount Hope shifted to the quarrying of stone for road and construction materials. This makes Mount Hope one of the oldest ongoing mining operations in the country.

Mount Hope went through several stages of development. In the early eighteenth century, the ore was for the taking from the vein outcroppings above the surface. The largest of these was the Great Jugular, later known as the Taylor Vein, which was said to have extended above ground more than one hundred feet.

It was not until the 1830s that the land became deeded and the early mining tracts were consolidated. The ore that was previously mined and sent to distant furnaces for smelting was now being processed at the many nearby forges that had opened up on the local rivers. In this preindustrial period, Mount Hope ironworkers lived on forge farms or iron plantations.

Iron Plantation

With the completion of the construction of the Ford–Faesch Ironmaster's House in 1772, Mount Hope became a fully integrated iron plantation. Under the guidance of John Jacob Faesch, the existing forges were consolidated under a new furnace. This furnace was most likely situated on the stream near the Mount Hope Methodist Church and operated until 1827. Faesch's operation supplied the Continental army with cast-iron products, including munitions, directly from the furnace as well as wrought-iron implements from the forges.

Industrial Revolution

The most far-reaching changes at Mount Hope came about as the result of the Industrial Revolution. In 1831, the Mount Hope Mining Company was incorporated, and with the opening of the Morris Canal, ore was once again shipped off site for processing. The mine's rich magnetite ores were prized by New Jersey and Pennsylvania ironworks because of their relative purity.

Mount Hope became a company town, shipping ore west to the steel mills in Pennsylvania's Lehigh Valley as well as locally. In this capacity, Mount Hope was an integral part of the iron-producing region stretching from the eastern Pennsylvania anthracite coal fields to the marketing and distribution centers of the metropolitan area. During this period, iron was mined in larger quantities at Mount Hope than ever before, but smelting (forging) no longer occurred on the site.

The 1850 Expansion

During this time, Mount Hope mining was acquired by Moses Taylor, a New York industrial financier, to provide an additional source of iron ore for his interest in the Scranton (Wyoming Valley) Pennsylvania area where the Lackawanna Iron and Coal Company was located. In its heyday, as many as nine veins were being worked simultaneously and a tramway was constructed to link the mine with the Morris Canal in nearby Rockaway.

MINING MOVES WEST

By the 1880s, the impact of the opening of the Mesabi Range in Minnesota and other midwestern mines was beginning to be felt. These huge strip-mining operations supplied iron ore at far less cost than the eastern mines. As coal mining moved west and transportation distances to the processing mills increased, the demand for eastern iron ore fell even more.

By the turn of the century, many of the less profitable eastern mines had closed and many of the remaining iron companies in New Jersey and Pennsylvania were consolidated into the Empire Iron and Steel Company in an effort to compete for the shrinking market for iron ore. Operations in the east continued at decreasing production levels until the depression when many mines, including Mount Hope, closed.

WORLD WAR II PROVIDES STIMULUS

The state-of-the-art New Leonard complex was constructed in 1942–43, and by 1950, Mount Hope under Shamoon Industries had surpassed all other New Jersey mines in the total production of iron ore. In 1959, the demand for ore fell once again and the mine closed. Throughout the 1960s, stockpiled ore and quarried rock was shipped from Mount Hope for highway and major commercial development in the New York Metropolitan area.

THE LEGACY

The physical setting and equipment of this historic mining complex represent a major portion of a significant industrial site of regional and national importance. Not only is the site one of the largest and most productive magnetite iron mines in America, but it is also the only remaining, virtually intact setting of mining structures in what was once an important national industrial resource.

Iron Industry in Morris County

Substantial above-ground remains of the Industrial Revolution are still evident at Mount Hope and include mining buildings, offices, the company store, an 1860s miners' church and the railroad spur that connected the mine with the Morris Canal and major trunk rail lines. Below-ground remains constitute another source of cultural resources. These include remains of buildings, ironworks and equipment along with the long-abandoned mines.

Appendix B

WASHINGTON'S
LOOKING GLASS

In the research of the Ford family, the following poem was found. Since it relates directly to a specific object still viewable on exhibit in the Ford mansion, it would be worthwhile to print it in full. While perhaps lacking in literary merit, it is nonetheless indicative of the types of pastimes engaged in—particularly by women—in the mid- to late nineteenth century. It would belong to a genre of poetry referred to as parlor poetry, as it was often written for and recited among friends while gathering in a parlor. The goal was not high art; rather the goal was entertainment and amusement through clever language or sentimental thoughts. This poem to the memory of Washington is symptomatic of this type of expressive, effusive and, in this case, approaching hagiographic poetry.

ON AN OLD MIRROR

Used by Washington, at his Headquarters, the Ford mansion, in Morristown, New Jersey, 1779–1780.

Old Mirror, speak, and tell us whence
Thou camest, and then, who brought thee hence,
Did dear old England give thee birth?
Or merry France, the land of mirth?
In vain another should we seek
At all like thee—thou thing antique.

Of the old Mansion thou seems't part;
Indeed, to me, its very heart;
For in thy face, though dimmed with age,
I read my country's brightest page.
Five generations all have passed,
And yet, Old Mirror, thou dost last:
The young, the old, the good, the bad,
The gay, the gifted, and the sad,
Are gone; their hopes, their sighs, their fears

Are buried deep with smiles and tears.
Then speak, old Mirror; thou hast seen
Full many a noble form, I ween;
Full many a soldier, tall and brave,
Now lying in a nameless grave;
Full many a fairy form and bright,
Have flitted by when hearts were light;
Full many a bride—whose short life seemed
Too happy to be even dreamed;
Full many a lord and titled dame,
Bearing full many an honored name;
And tell us, Mirror, how they dressed,
Those stately dames, when in their best?
If robes and sacques the damsels wore,
And sweeping skirts in days of yore?
But tell us, too, for we must hear
Of him whom all the world revere.
Thou sawest him when the times so dark
Had made upon his brow their mark,
Those fearful times, those dreary days,
When all seemed but a tangled maze,
His noble army, worn with tolls,
Giving their life-blood to the soils,
Disease and famine brooding o'er;
His Country's foe e'en at his door;
But ever saw him noble, brave,
Seeking her freedom or his grave.
His was the heart that never quailed;
His was the arm that never failed!

Old Mirror! Thou hast seen what we
Would barter all most dear to see;
The great, the good, the noblest one
Our own Immortal Washington!
Well may we gaze—for ne'er again
Old Mirror, shall we see such men;
And when we, too, have lived our day,
Like those before us passed away,
Still, valued Mirror, mayest thou last
To tell our children of the past;
Still thy dimmed face, thy tarnished frame,
Why honored house and time proclaim;
And ne'er may sacrilegious hand,
While Freedom claims it as her land;
One stone or pebble rashly throw
To lay thee, honored Mirror, low.

—T.F.

This poem is believed to have been written by one of Gabriel Ford's daughter-in-law sometime after the Civil War but prior to the auction in 1873.

FIRE INSURANCE APPLICATION
OF HENRY A. FORD

Application of Henry A. Ford of the township of Morris, county of Morris New Jersey to the Rahway Mutual Fire Insurance Company for Insurance against loss by Fire for the term of __ years, for the sum of Three Thousand Dollars on the following property, to wit, on his double two story Dwelling house, Kitchen & Shed or Leanto in Morristown, hereinafter more particularly described.

Estimated value	$12000 [18000?]
Amount proposed for Insurance	3000
Amount of Premium Note	240
Amount of Cash	30

Said Dwelling House &c is situated in Morristown N. Jersey, about three quarters of a mile from the Morris Green, near the junction of the Turnpike Road leading to Elizabeth Town & the road leading to Whippany and is commonly called "Washington's Headquarters" late the residence of the Honl. Gabriel H. Ford deceased, now owned & occupied by Applicant, as his family Residence.

The Buildings are principally of wood, though generally filled in with Brick, except the Shed or Leanto & are in good tenantable condition having been lately about the year 1853, thoroughly repaired & painted outside & in &c.

The size of the main building is about fifty four feet front, by about thirty two feet deep, two stories high, with good cellar underneath the whole [and]

Garret above, not finished off. A wide Hall through on the lower or first floor, on which are four rooms, two on each side of the Hall, with stair way, leading to the Second Story. On the Second Story floor there are five bed rooms, besides a Hall common to them, & from which there is a closet [closed?] stair way to the Garret above the whole.

The Kitchen or Wing is also two stories high but not of the height of the Main building & is about thirty two feet in front by about twenty seven feet deep. On the lower floor is a Hall or Rutder [?] from front to rear, the Main Kitchen Room and two small apartments,—one used Ordinarily as a store room & the other as a pantry. There is a stair way leading from the entry & taken off of it to the Second Story, on which are five bed rooms besides passages, from one of which is a stair way to the Garret above which is unfinished. By this Stair way there is also a communication with the back room of the Main building giving access to & from the Main building & Wing. There is also a passage way from the Kitchen below to the Leanto & from this passageway a narrow stair way to one of the back bedrooms above.

The Shed or Leanto is in rear of the Kitchen & is about nineteen feet long by about ten feet wide.

There are two chimneys to the Main building and one to the Wing or Kitchen. In the Main building there were originally seven fireplaces, but these have been closed up with Brick &c., with Stove pipe aperture at each except one (the parlor) in which there is a Coal Grate. It being the intention to use (optionally) at each of the others, stoves for wood or coal, and a stove for wood or coal in the back room on the first floor of the Main building, used occasionally as a Bedroom and Library & Office. There is a large Range &[?] stove for coal or wood in the principal Hall, with pipe passing through the Ceiling, guardedly to the Hall above into a Drum there & from there [?] through a partition also guardedly into one of the back rooms where it, where it [*sic*] communicates Carefully with the Stack of the chimney.

There is a Cooking range in the Kitchen with an Oven attached, beside a Common brick oven underneath which is a safe place for wood ash [bin?] & in the Kitchen are the Water arrangements of Copper Boiler &c.

All the buildings are covered with Shingles & there are lightning rods terminating at each of the Chimneys.

There were two Stone cisterns formerly in use near the Kitchen door for rain water, but these have been in a measure neglected & one out of use, the premises being supplied with spring water [from a distance?] by means of a Hydraulic Ram which sends a supply into a large Tank holding many barrels in the Kitchen Garret from which it is carried to a Bath room below laden off of one of the Kitchen bed rooms & thereto in the Kitchen to the Kitchen fixtures & improvements below.

This application and term being some but not very essentially for [from?] my written application to the Company on or about the 24. Decr. 1853, and from my after Statement written to the Company on or about the 26. March 1860[?], to both of which I here refer.

There is Insurance of the premises with Newark Mutual Fire Association Company of Two thousand Eight hundred dollars ($2800). Policy ending 23d Septemr. 1863. Also in the Bergen County Farmers Mutual Fire Insurance Company for Two Hundred Dollars ($200). Policy ending March 2nd 1865.

Henry A. Ford
Applicant

Source: Morristown National Historical Park Library; Ford Family Papers, 1738/9–1904; book 9, series 2; box 4, folder 2.

THE IRON MINES OF
MORRIS COUNTY

T he following two charts were compiled by Kevin Perry for an exhibit
prepared by the Morris County Historical Society.

Town	Mine Name	Approx. Date	Owner/ Operator	Production	Supplied Ore To
Boonton Township	Botts Farm Mine	1872–1890	W.S. DeCamp	Exploratory	
	Rockaway Valley/ DeCamp Mines	1820–1887	W.S. DeCamp, leased to Musconetcong Iron Works	500 tons	
Chester Township	Barnes Mine	1864–1887	J.M.D. Barnes	several thousand tons	Stanhope Furnace
	Beemer Mine	1866–1887	various, leased by Bethlehem Iron Co.	several thousand tons	
	Blauvelt Mine	1890	Wiggins and Henderson	2,400 tons	Pennsylvania furnaces
	Budd Mine	1865–1887	Daniel Budd, later operated by Cooper Mining Co.	several thousand tons	
	Chester Mine/ George Shaft	1881		400 tons	
	Child Mine	1874	L. Child	Exploratory	

Town	Mine Name	Approx. Date	Owner/ Operator	Production	Supplied Ore To
	Collis Farm Exploration	1873		Exploratory	
	Cooper Mine	1868–1886	Cooper Mining Co.	approx. 120,000 tons	
	Creager/Peach Orchard Mine	1868–1887			
	Cramer/ Creamer	1868–1873		Exploratory	
	Cromwell/ Chester Highland Mine	1872–1890	Chester Highland Mining Company		Chester Furnace, Pennsylvania
	De Camp Mine	1869–1874		Exploratory	
	Dickerson Farm Mine	1868–1890	Seals and Thomas	several thousand tons	Crane Iron Co.
	Gulick Farm Mines	1867–1887	Cooper Mining Co.	several thousand tons	Pennsylvania
	Hacklebarney Mines	1760–1896	Chester Iron Co./Andover Iron Co.	tens of thousands of tons	Pennsylvania
	Harden Mine	1869	C. Harden	Exploratory	
	Hedges Mine	1870–1883	William J. Taylor, Union Iron Co., North Jersey Iron Co.		
	Horton Mine	1867–1870		4,000 tons	
	Hotel Mine	1870–1890			
	Kean Mine				
	Leake/Leek Mine	1866–1887	Bethlehem Iron Co.		
	Pitney Mine	1873–1881	Cooper, Hewitt & Co.	several thousand tons	Pequest furnace
	Quimby Mine	1880s–1890			
	Rarick Farm Explorations	1870–1879		various explorations	

The Iron Mines of Morris County

Town	Mine Name	Approx. Date	Owner/ Operator	Production	Supplied Ore To
	Sampson/ Samson/ Skellenger Mine	1867– 1890	Cooper, Hewitt & Co.	several thousand tons	Pennsylvania
	Skellenger Mine	1881– 1882			
	Squier's/ Squire's Mine	1880– 1890		Exploratory	
	Swayze/ Sweayze Mine	1868– 1887	Andover Mining Company	several thousand tons	
	Thorp/ Throop Mine	1887– 1890		minimal production	
	Tiger Mine	1868– 1887		minimal production	
	Topping Mine	1868– 1887	William J. Taylor & Co.		Chester Furnace
	Woodhull Mine	1868– 1873	leased to John Webb Jr., later Ario Pardee	minimal production	
	Wortman Mine	1873– 1890		minimal production	
Hanover	Beers Mine	1878– 1880		minimal production	
Jefferson Township	Davenport Mine	1868– 1887		minimal production	
	Dodge Mine	1853– 1910	various, including Bethlehem Iron Co., Phelps, Dodge & Co., Jefferson Iron Co.		
	Ford/Headley Mine	1853– 1874	Glendon Iron Work, Glendon Iron Co., Musconetcong Iron Co.	tens of thousands of tons	
	Duffee/Megie Mine	1841– 1869			

Town	Mine Name	Approx. Date	Owner/ Operator	Production	Supplied Ore To
	Fraser/Frazer Mine	1867–1880		Exploratory	
	Hurd/ Hurdtown Mine	1804–1910	Hurd Family, Glendon Iron Co., Hurd Mining Company	tens of thousands of tons	Pennsylvania furnaces
	Hurdtown/ Apatite Mine	1790–1880	Hurd Family		
	Nolans Mine	1796–1880	Nolan family, Ogden Mine Co.		
	Scofield/ Schofield Mine	1807–1890	various, leased by Trenton Iron Co., sold to Lehigh Crane Iron Co.	tens of thousands of tons	Pennsylvania
	Weldon Mines (Upper/ Lower)	1775–1920	Ford, DeCamp, Blackwell & McFarlan, Hopping, Weldon Iron Mining Co., etc.	tens of thousands of tons	
	aka Hopping, Jonah, Heckscher-Weldon				
	Copley-Weldon				
Kinnelon	Cole Farm Exploration	1874		Exploratory	
	Gould's Farm Mine	1873		Exploratory	
	Stony Brook/ Pike's Peak Mine	1768–1880	London Co., Martin J. Ryerson		Bloomingdale
	Connet/Water Street Mine	1868–1875			
Mendham	Lewis/Herrick Mine	1868–1887			

The Iron Mines of Morris County

Town	Mine Name	Approx. Date	Owner/ Operator	Production	Supplied Ore To
Mine Hill Township	Baker/Crane Mines	1847–1891	H. & W.H. Baker Iron Mines, Crane Iron Co., Lackawanna Iron & Coal, Joseph Wharton	tens of thousands of tons	Local and Pennsylvania
	Black Hills Mine	1879–1905	Dickerson-Suckasunny Mining Co.	several thousand tons	Seacaucus Iron Works
	Brotheron & Byram Mines	1842–1901	John Byram, Dover Iron Co., Andover Iron Co., George & Pullman	tens of thousands of tons	
	Canfield Mine	1868–1890	Dickerson-Suckasunny Mining Co.	25,000 tons	
	Canfield's Phosphatic Iron Mine	1870–1891		Exploratory	
	Dickerson/ Succasunna Mines	1713–1908	Mahlon Dickerson, Dickerson Suckasunny Mining Co., Allentown Iron Co., E. Canfield & Co.		
			Ario Pardee, Musconetcong Iron Co., Succasunna Iron Co.	tens of thousands of tons	Morris County forges, Stanhope furnaces
					Musconetcong Iron Works
	Erb Mine	1868–1891	Andover Iron Co.		Pennsylvania furnaces
	Evers Mine	1868–1883	Saucon Iron Co.		Saucon Iron Co. furnace in PA

Town	Mine Name	Approx. Date	Owner/ Operator	Production	Supplied Ore To
	King Mine	1853–1880		10,000 tons	
	Millen/ Mellon/ Mellen/Millon	1850–1890	Green & Dennison, Fuller & Lord, Boonton Iron Co.	several thousand tons	Boonton & Port Oram (Wharton)
	Randall Hill Mine	1855–1887	Crane Iron Co.	several thousand tons	
	Scrub Oaks/ Dell Mines	1850s–1966	Cooper & Hewitt, Andover Iron Co., Edison Co., Wharton Steel Co., Replogle Steel Co.	over three million tons	
			Alan Wood Steel Co.		
Montville Township	Decker Mine	1872–1887		Exploratory	
	Taylor Mine	1858–1873		minimal production	Ringwood
Mount Arlington	Burt Mine	?-1880s		minimal production	
	Gove Mine	1868–1881	Francis M. Gove	several thousand tons	Pennsylvania
	Silver Spring Mine	1882–1887		minimal production	
Mount Olive	Appleget/ Applegit/ Applegate Mine	1880		minimal production	
	Cramer/ Creamer Mine	1850s–1890			
	Drake & Yager Mines	1848–1886	Musconetcong Iron Works, A.A. Drake Iron Co., Mount Olive Iron Co.	several thousand tons	

The Iron Mines of Morris County

Town	Mine Name	Approx. Date	Owner/ Operator	Production	Supplied Ore To
	Lowrance/ Lawrence Mine	1850s		likely never worked	
	Osborn Mine	1848–1890	A.A. Drake		
	Salmon/ Solomon's/ Soloman/ Mount Olive Mine	1846–1886	Crane Iron Co., Musconetcong Iron Co., Lehigh Crane Iron Co., Mount Olive Iron Co.	several thousand tons	Pennsylvania
			National Iron Co., Wynokie Iron Mining Co.		
	Shouse Mine	1879		Exploratory	
	Smith Mine	1850–1887		minimal production	Sparta forge
	Stephens/ Stevens Mine	1848–1887		minimal production	
Pequannock/ Montville	Kahart Mine	1868–1880		minimal production	
Randolph	Bryant/ Briant/Brant Mine	1868–1880s	Bryant family, Musconetcong Iron Co., Bethlehem Iron Co.	tens of thousands of tons	Pennsylvania
	Combs & Skellenger Mines	1828–1890	Thomas Reynolds, E. Canfield		Scranton, Pennsylvania
	Cooper Mine	1870			
	Dalrymple/ Carbon Mine	1860s–1916	Carbon Iron Co., Crane Iron Co.	tens of thousands of tons	Pennsylvania
	DeHart & Gordon/ Lawrence Mines	1864–1890	Reading Iron Co.		Pennsylvania

Town	Mine Name	Approx. Date	Owner/ Operator	Production	Supplied Ore To
	Fowland/ Follon/ Foulon/ Farland Mine	1860s– 1887			
	Frenchman's Mine				
	George Mine	1855– 1873			
	Henderson Mine	1867– 1870s	Dorastus Bryant	minimal production	
	(David) Horton Mine	pre 1868– 1873		minimal production	
	Jackson Hill Mine	1772– 1876	John J. Faesch, Robert F. Oram, Green & Dennison	100,000 tons	
	Charles King Mine	pre 1868– 1870		minimal production	
	Munson Mine	1859– 1890			
	Trowbridge Mine	pre 1868		Exploratory	
	De Bow/ Miller Mine	1872– 1906			
	Jackson/ Axtell/ Pompton Mine	1862– 1874			
	Lanagan Mine	1868– 1890		minimal production	
	Ryerson Debow/Bishop & Search Mine	1872– 1906		minimal production	Seacaucus
Rockaway	Allen Mine	1700s– 1918	John J. Faesch, Canfield & Losey, Joseph & William Jackson, Andover Iron Co.	tens of thousands of tons	

The Iron Mines of Morris County

Town	Mine Name	Approx. Date	Owner/ Operator	Production	Supplied Ore To
			New Jersey Iron Mining Co., Wharton Steel Co., Thomas Iron Co.		
	Baker Mine	1866–1906	William & Henry Baker, Allentown Iron Co.	400,000 tons	
	Beach Mine	1785–1886	Hibernia Iron Mining Co., Glendon Iron Co., NJ Iron Mining Co., Andover Iron Co.		
	Beach Glen Mine	1751–1930	Boonton Iron Co., J. Cooper Lord, Beach Glen Mining Co., Joseph Wharton		
	Birch Mine			minimal production	
	Bush Mine	1937	Warren Foundry and Pipe Co.	Exploratory	
	Canfield/ Pardee Mutual Mines	1776–1890	Job Allen, William S. DeCamp, Green Pond Iron Mining Co., Chester Iron Co.	tens of thousands of tons	
	Charlottesburg Mine	1760s–1888	Job Allen, William DeCamp, Green Pond Iron Mining Co., Cooper, Hewitt & Co.	tens of thousands of tons	

Town	Mine Name	Approx. Date	Owner/ Operator	Production	Supplied Ore To
	Chester Iron Co. Mines	1776–1890	Job Allen, William DeCamp, Green Pond Iron Mining Co., Chester Iron Co.	tens of thousands of tons	
	Cobb/Split Rock Mine	1860s–1890	Andrew B. Cobb, William D. Marvel	several thousand tons	Split Rock Forge
	Cogill/ Cogswell Mine	1833–1910	John Righter, Musconetcong Iron Works, Elliott Mining Co., Coggill Iron Co.		
	Copperas Mine	1700s–1872	Thomas Young		
	Crane/ Glendon/Scott Mines	1700s–1917	Jacksons, Glendon Iron Co., Joseph Wharton, Replogle Steel		
	Davenport Mine	1882–1884		Exploratory	
	DeCamp Mine	1700s–1917	Edward DeCamp, Glendon Iron Co., NJ Iron Mining Co., Joseph Wharton, Replogle Steel		
	Denmark Mine	1887		minimal production	
	Dolan Mine	1869–1890	Crane Iron Co., Joseph Wharton	minimal production	
	Gidd/Beach Mine	1868–1887	NJ Iron Mining Co., Andover Iron Co., Musconetcong Iron Co.		

The Iron Mines of Morris County

Town	Mine Name	Approx. Date	Owner/ Operator	Production	Supplied Ore To
	Green Pond Mines	1872–1899	Green Pond Iron Mining Co.	50,000 tons	
	Howell Tract Mine	1874–1886	Mutual Iron Co.	minimal production	
	Kitchell/Wild Cat Mine	pre 1873–1890	Kitchell Mining Co.	minimal production	
	Meriden Mine	pre 1868–1890			
	Mount Hope Mines	1700s–1978	Jacob Ford, Mount Hope Iron Co., Lackawanna Iron and Coal Co., Empire Steel & Iron Co.		Local and Pennsylvania
			Replogle Steel, Shamoon Industries		
	Old Ford/ Horse Pond/ Church Mine	1700s–1880s	Samuel Ford, Glendon Iron Co.		
	Richard Mine	1700s–1930	John J. Faesch, Dover Co., Blackwell & McFarlan, Thomas Iron Co.		Local and Pennsylvania
	Teabo Mine	1700s–1918	John J. Faesch, Canfield & Losey, Glendon Iron Co., Wharton Steel		
	Theo./Lower Wood Mine	1700s–1917	Beach Family, Andover Iron Co., NJ Iron Mining Co., Joseph Wharton, Replogle Steel		Local and Pennsylvania

Town	Mine Name	Approx. Date	Owner/ Operator	Production	Supplied Ore To
	Tichenor Mine				
	Upper Wood Mine	1700s– 1917	Glendon Iron Works, NJ Iron Mining Co., Joseph Wharton, Replogle Steel		
	Willis & Cobb/ Wharton Mine	1700s– 1917	Glendon Iron Col, NJ Iron Mining Co., Bethlehem Iron Co., Joseph Wharton, Replogle Steel		
	White Meadow Mines	pre 1840– 1890	Boonton Iron Co.		
Roxbury	Baptist Church Mine	1873– 1887		minimal production	
	High Ledge Mine	1868– 1890			
	Hilts Mine	1854– 1890	Crane Iron Co.		
	King Mine	1868– 1905			
	Lake View Mine	1863– 1882		minimal production	
	Lurk Mine	1904		Wharton Furnace	
	Stanhope Mine	1795– 1856	Jonathon Dickerson		
	Wolfe Mine	1880– 1901		minimal production	
Washington Township	Fisher/ Beatyestown Mine	1864– 1887		tens of thousands of tons	
	Hann/Hahn/ Kann Mine	1871– 1887		several thousand tons	
	Hopler/ Bartleyville Mine	1868– 1887	Thomas Iron Co.	minimal production	

The Iron Mines of Morris County

Town	Mine Name	Approx. Date	Owner/ Operator	Production	Supplied Ore To
	Langdon Mine	1879–1890	L.W. Langdon & Son		
	Marsh/Youngs Mine	1832–1887	W.W. Marsh	local	
	Naughright Mine	1870–1887	D. Runkle & Co.		
	Sharp Mine	1871–1890		minimal production	
	Stoutenberg Mine	1868–1890		minimal production	Hackettstown Furnace
Wharton	Hoff/Huff Mine	1800s–1913	Chester Iron Co., Andover Iron Co., Oram, Hance & Co.	tens of thousands of tons	
	Johnson Hill Mine	1868–1890			
	Meadow/Bull Frog Mine	1868–1887	Carbon Iron Co., J. Cooper Lord Estate	tens of thousands of tons	
	Mount Pleasant Mine	1786–1890	Moses Tuttle, Guy Hinchman, Dennison & Green, Fuller & Lord, Mount Pleasant Mining Co.		
	Orchard Mine	1849–1908	Green & Dennison, Fuller & Lord		Boonton Iron Works, Pennsylvania
	West Mount Pleasant Mine	1868–1887	Hoff & Hoagland, Carbon Iron Co.		

FORGES AND FURNACES OF MORRIS COUNTY

Location	Name	Years of Operation	Original Owner/ Operator
	Bloomingdale Furnace	1740	Ogdens of Newark
Boonton	Boonton Forge	1759–1829	David Ogden
	Boonton Iron Works	1830–1890	New Jersey Iron Company
	Deeker's/Decker's Forge	1825–?	John Decker
	Dixon's Forge	1830–	James Dixon
	Powerville Rolling Mill	1846 as part of Powerville Forge	Elijah Scott & Thomas C. Willis
	Powerville Forge/ Scott's Forge	1794–1880s	Joseph Scott
Chester	Chester Furnace	1878	Unknown
	Hacklebarney Forge	1763–?	Christopher Beekman
Denville	Coleraine (Cold-rain) Forge	pre-1760–early 1800s	Unknown
	Franklin Forge	pre-1760–1850s	John Cobb, Thomas Brown & Stephen Jackson
	Ninkey/Losey's Forge	pre-1760–early 1800s	Unknown
Dover	Dover Iron Works, Rolling Mill, Slitting Mill	1792–1922	Josiah Beman, Israel Canfield, Jacob Losey
	Jackson's Forge	1722–?	John Jackson
	Morris County Machine & Iron Co. Foundry & Machine Shop	1868	George Richards
	Quaker Iron Works (became Dover Iron Works)	1745–1792	Joseph Shotwell
Hanover	Malapardis/Stony Brook Forge	1765–1800	Unknown

The Iron Mines of Morris County

Location	Name	Years of Operation	Original Owner/ Operator
Jefferson Township	Cobb & Bigalow's Forge/Squire Cobb's/Bigalow & Deeker's/Tobacco	1840–1880s	Unknown
	Hard Bargain Forge	late 1700s–1880s	John Dow, Christian Strait, John Davenport, Cornelius Davenport
	Hopewell/ Upper Farmingham Forge	late 1700s–1850s	Samuel Ogden
	Hurd/ Two Partners Forge	1790–1800s	Daniel & Joseph Hurd
	Lower Longwood Forge	1796–1860s	Ebenezer Tuttle & Grandin Morris
	Petersburg Forge/ Arnold's Iron Works	1730–1850s	Unknown
	Russia/Lower Farmingham/ William Headley's Forge	1700s–1880s	Unknown
	Swedeland/Milton Forge	1797–1880s	John Dow, Cornelius Davenport & Jacob Ryker
	Upper Longwood Forge	1700s–1860s	Unknown, rebuilt in 1798 by John DeCamp
	Weldon Forge	1800–?	Moses Hopping
	Woodstock Forge	1823–1890s	Ephraim Adams, James L. Dickerson & Stephen Adams
Kinnelon	Montgomery/ Stony Brook Forge	1821–1850s	Hubbard S. Stickle
Mendham	Liddle's Forge	1700s–early 1800s	William Liddle
	Mendham Forge	Unknown	Unknown
	Rushe's Forge	pre-1786–1820s	Michael Rushe
	Rye/ Axtell Forge	late 1700s	Unknown
Morris Plains	Hathaway Forge	1700s–1820s	James Keen
Morristown	Ford Forge	1700s–1823	Jacob Ford, Sr.
	Speedwell Splitting Mill/ Forge	pre-1800	Unknown

Location	Name	Years of Operation	Original Owner/ Operator
	Speedwell Iron Works	1815	Stephen Vail, William Campfield, Isaac Canfield
Mount Olive	Casterline's Forge	1700s	Unknown
	Crane Iron Company (numerous owners/ names)	1846	Unknown
	Eaton/Heaton Forge	1734–1750s	Samuel Heaton
	Hinchman's Forge	1802–1850s	William Hinchman
	Mount Olive Bloomery	1700s	Samuel Heaton
	Stanhope Furnaces	1780–1840	Upper Forge built by Silas Dickerson, Lower Forge built by David S. Canfield
	Stephens Furnace	1840–1870s	William A. Stephens
	Welsh/Welch Forge	1790–1840?	Original Builder Unknown, became site of Bartley Foundry
Parsippany	Troy/Cobb's Forge	1743–?	John Cobb
Randolph	Shongum/Young's Forge	1756–1820s	Robert Young & Robert Young, Jr.
Rockaway	Adventure Furnace & Forge aka Hibernia	1763–	Samuel Ford
	Beach Glen Forge/ Johnston Iron Works/ Horse Pond Forge	1751–1860s	John Johnston
	Beman's/White Meadow/Muir Forge	1753–1820s	David Beman & Thomas Miller
	Denmark/Burnt Meadow Forge	1750–1860s?	Jacob Ford
	Durham Forge	1800–1856	Ebenezer Cobb
	Guinea or Muir's Forge	pre-1774–?	Colonel John Munson & Benjamin Beach
	Hibernia Forge	1821–1850s	William Scott, replaced Furnace
	Job Allen's Iron Works/Upper Forge at Rockaway	1730–1890s	Job Allen

Location	Name	Years of Operation	Original Owner/ Operator
	Johnston's Iron Works/Horse Pound Forge/Beach Glen Bloomery	1753–1860s	John Johnston
	Lower Forge at Rockaway	1795–1820	Stephen Jackson, later site of Rolling Mill
	Middle or Aetna Forge	1749–1880s	Jonathan Osborn
	Mount Hope Furnace	1772–1827	John Jacob Faesch
	Mount Pleasant Forges	1750–1850s	Colonel Jacob Ford Sr.
	Rockaway Rolling Mills/Furnace	1822–1887	Joseph & William Jackson
	Split Rock/Dixon's Forge	1790–1850s	Ebenezer Farrand, later site of Split Rock Furnace
	Split Rock Furnace	1862	Andrew B. Cobb
	Timber Brook Forge	1821–1850s	John Dow
	Meriden Forges	1789–1900s	? Farrand
	Union Foundry	1845–1887?	James Fulller & Mahlon Hoagland
Roxbury	Boston Forge	1700s	Unknown
	Brookland/Brooklyn Forge	1764–1820s	Benjamin & Thomas Coe
	Valley Forge	1780–1875	Jared Coe & Minard Lefever
Washington Township	Bartley Foundry	1790–1862	Unknown
Wharton	Port Oram Furnace	1868–1920s	John Cooper Lord, Robert F. Oram, et al
	Washington Forge	pre-1795–1880?	Unknown
Whippany	Old Forge	1710–mid-1700s	Unknown, tradition records it built by John Ford & John Budd
Whippany River	Carmichael Forge	Between 1750–1776	Unknown
	Whippany Bloomery	post–1710	Unknown

Appendix E

THE GEOLOGY OF
NEW JERSEY

For an area of its size, New Jersey has a unique and interesting geology.[147] The state can be divided into four regions, known as physiographic provinces, which have distinctive rocks and landforms.

The Valley and Ridge Province is underlain by faulted and folded sedimentary layers of sandstone, shale and limestone that range in age from Cambrian to Devonian (570 to 345 million years old). These rocks originated as sand, mud and lime sediment deposited in former seas and floodplains. During Ordovician time (approximately 450 million years ago) and again during Pennsylvanian and Permian time (approximately 300 million years ago), the rocks were deformed by compression into folds and thrust along faults. As a result of the deformation, the originally flat sedimentary layers were tilted and now outcrop as linear belts.

Alternation of belts of erosion-resistant sandstone and easily eroded shale and limestone creates the long, parallel northeast–southwest trending ridges and valleys characteristic of the province. Resistant sandstone and siltstone layers underlie Kittatinny Mountain and Walpack Ridge; shale and limestone underlie the valley of Flat Brook, the Delaware Valley upstream from the Delaware Water Gap, and the broad valley between Kittatinny Mountain and the Highlands to the east.

The limestone is quarried for construction material and cement aggregate. Some of the limestone units yield large quantities of ground water. The shale and sandstones and some limestone units are generally less productive aquifers.

One the eastern edge of the Valley and Ridge Province, along a line from Franklin through Andover to the Delaware River just north of

Phillipsburg, an irregular escarpment averaging five hundred feet in height marks the boundary of the Highlands Province. The Highlands are underlain predominantly by granite, gneiss and small amounts of marble of Precambrian age. These rocks, the oldest in New Jersey, were formed between 1.3 billion and 750 million years ago by melting and recrystalization of sedimentary rocks that were deeply buried, subjected to high pressure and temperature and intensely deformed. The Precambrian rocks are interrupted by several elongate northeast–southwest trending belts of folded Paleozoic sedimentary rocks equivalent to the rocks of the Valley and Ridge Province.

The granites and gneisses are resistant to erosion and create a hilly upland dissected by the deep, steep-sided valleys of major streams. The belts of sedimentary rock form long, parallel ridges and valleys (for example, Bearfort Mountain, Long Valley and the Musconetcong Valley) that extend through the province.

The Highlands contain magnetite iron ore deposits that formerly supplied an industry of national importance. A valuable and mineralogically unique zinc ore in the Franklin Marble at Ogdensburg was also mined. In places the rocks of the Highlands are quarried for crushed stone. The Precambrian rocks are generally unproductive aquifers except where they are fractured or weathered. The more productive aquifers of the region are the glacial deposits and some of the Paleozoic sedimentary rocks.

Rocks of Piedmont Province are separated from the rocks of the Highlands Province by a series of major faults, including the Ramapo Fault. The more resistant gneisses and granites on the up thrown northwest side of the faults make a prominent escarpment, two hundred to eight hundred feet in height, extending from Mahwah through Boonton and Morristown to Gladstone, and form there westward in an irregular line to the Delaware River near Milford.

South and east of this escarpment, interbedded sandstone, shale, conglomerate, basalt and disbase of the Piedmont Province underlie a broad lowland interrupted by long, generally northeast–southwest treading ridges and uplands. The rocks of the Piedmont are of Late Triassic and Early Jurassic age (230 to 190 million years old). They rest on a large, elongate crustal block that dropped downward in the initial stages of the opening of the Atlantic Ocean—one of a series of such blocks in eastern North America. These down-dropped blocks formed valleys known as rift basins. Sediment eroded from adjacent uplands was deposited along rivers and in lakes within the basins. These sediments became compacted and cemented to form conglomerate, sandstone, siltstone, and shale. They commonly have a distinctive reddish-brown color.

The Geology of New Jersey

In the course of rifting, the rock layers of the Piedmont became tilted northwestward, gently folded and cut by several major faults. Volcanic activity was also associated with the rifting, as indicated by the basalt and diabase interlayer with the sandstone and shale. Diabase is a rock formed by the cooling of magma at some depth in the crust; basalt is formed by cooling of an identical magma that has been extruded onto the surface as lava. Both basalt and diabase are more resistant to erosion than the enclosing sandstone and shale and therefore they form ridges and uplands. The Palisades, Rocky Hill, Sourland Mountain and Cushetunk Mountain are underlain by disbase layers. The Watchung Mountains, Long Hill and Hook Mountain are underlain by basalt layers. Valleys and lowlands between these ridges are underlain by shale and sandstone.

The basalt and diabase are extensively quarried for crushed stone. In the past, "brownstone" was widely quarried from sandstone units. Also, minor quantities of copper were extracted from sandstone and shale associated with the diabase and basalt. The basalt and diabase generally are poor aquifers but the sedimentary rocks are, in places, capable of yielding large quantities of water.

Southeast of a line roughly between Carteret and Trenton, unconsolidated sediments of the Coastal Plain Province overlap rocks of the Piedmont Province. These sediments, which range in age from Cretaceous to Miocene (135 to 5.3 million years old), dip toward the coast and extent beneath the Atlantic Ocean to the edge of the Continental Shelf. The Coastal Plain sediments thicken southeastward from a featheredge along the northwestern margin of the province to approximately 4,500 feet near Atlantic City to a maximum of more than 40,000 feet in the area of the Baltimore Canyon Trough, 50 miles offshore from Atlantic City. The sediments consist of layers of sand, silt and clay deposited alternately in deltaic and marine environments as sea level fluctuated during Cretaceous and Tertiary time. These layers of sediment outcrop in irregular bands that trend northeast–southwest. Wide areas of the Coastal Plain are covered by a thin veneer of Late Tertiary and Quatemary sand and gravel deposited by rivers.

The topography of the Coastal Plain generally is flat to very gently undulating. However, erosion-resistant gravel or iron-cemented sediment underlie upland areas and isolated hills, such as the Atlantic Highlands, Telegraphy Hill, Mount Holly and Arneys Mount.

Coastal Plain sediments have been mined in the past for bog iron, glass sand, foundry sand, ceramic and brick clay, the mineral glauconite for use in fertilizer, and clay and titanium from the mineral ilmenite in sand deposits.

Today the Coastal Plain sediments continue to supply glass sand and are extensively mined for sand and gravel construction material. The sand formations are productive aquifers and important groundwater reservoirs.

Within each of these physiographic provinces there have been major changes during the past two million years. In this time, New Jersey has undergone three glaciations. The last glacier (the late Wisconsinan advance) began to melt back from its maximum extent approximately twenty thousand years ago. North of the limit of the last glaciation much of the surface is covered by glacial deposits. Upland areas in this region are thinly draped with till, an unsorted mixture of sand, clay and boulders deposited directly from glacier. Valleys and lowlands are filled with up to 350 feet of sand and gravel deposited from glacial melt water and silt and clay that settled in glacial lakes. The sand and gravel deposits are important sources of construction material, and productive aquifers are found where sand and gravel occur in buried or filled valleys. South of the limit of Wisconsinan glaciation, there are discontinuous patches of till from older glaciations. These deposits occur on uplands and are found as far south as the Somerville area.

During each glaciation, sea level dropped as water from the oceans was transferred to ice sheets. Rivers extended and deepened their valleys to conform to the lower sea levels. When the ice sheets melted, sea level rose, flooding the deepened valleys and establishing new shorelines. The present configuration of the coast is the result of the rapid post-glacial rise in sea level, which slowed approximately six thousand years ago. Many of the estuaries along the coast are the drowned lower reaches of former river valleys. To the east of the mainland, barrier islands were formed and continue to be shaped by erosion and deposition of beach sand by waves and currents. Mud and sand transported by rivers and from offshore is gradually filling the bays and estuaries between the mainland and the barrier islands, creating extensive wetlands.

Notes

Preface

1. Even within New Jersey, the Fords were not of the aristocratic class, however artificial that designation was. At no time did a Ford sit on the council or board of East Jersey—the typical place for the well-to-do to be.

Introduction

2. Morristown National Historical Park Cultural Landscape Report for Washington's Headquarters 2005. National Park Service, Olmsted Center for Landscape Preservation, Boston, 15.
3. For more information on the Ford Mansion, see Jude Pfister, *The Jacob Ford Jr. Mansion; the Storied History of a New Jersey Home* (Charleston: The History Press, 2009).
4. Vera B. Craig and Ralph H. Lewis, "Furnishings Plan for the Ford Mansion (1779–1780)," Morristown National Historical Park, 1976, 22.
5. William U. Massey, "Historical Grounds survey of Washington's Headquarters, The Ford Mansion Morristown, New Jersey." May 1975, 4.
6. In the *Jacob Ford Jr. Mansion*, Mrs. Ford's date of death is incorrectly listed as 1826. In fact, it was August 31, 1824. The author regrets this error.
7. Theodore Thayer, *Colonial and Revolutionary Morris County* (Morristown, NJ: Morris County Heritage Commission, 1975), 90–91.
8. The Colony of New Jersey was originally divided between West and East Jersey. West Jersey was the generally barren part of the state that had little population. East Jersey was considered very productive and had a vibrant population. During the Revolution, New Jersey officially became one.

9. Morristown National Historical Park Cultural Landscape Report for Washington's Headquarters (CLR), 2005, 13–14. National Park Service, Olmsted Center for Landscape Preservation, Boston, MA.

10. Thayer, *Colonial and Revolutionary*, 33.

11. Ibid., 34.

12. Ibid.

EIGHTEENTH-CENTURY NEW JERSEY

13. John E. Pomfret, *The Province of East New Jersey 1609–1702: The Rebellious Proprietary* (Princeton: Princeton University Press, 1962), viii. Governor Carteret was a cousin of the original grantee, Sir George Carteret.

14. Edgar Jacob Fisher, *New Jersey as a Royal Province 1738 to 1776* (New York: Columbia University, 1911), 171.

15. Pomfret, *Province of East New Jersey*, viii.

16. Ibid.

17. Ibid., 347.

18. Edgar Jacob Fisher, *New Jersey As a Royal Province 1738 to 1776* (New York: Columbia University, 1911), 171.

19. Pomfret, *Province of East New Jersey*, 361.

20. Fisher, *New Jersey*, 171.

21. Ibid., 172.

22. Ibid.

23. Ibid.

24. Emily W.B. Russell, "Vegetation of Northern New Jersey Before European Settlement," *American Midland Naturalist* 105, no. 1 (January 1981): 10.

25. Ibid., 5.

26. Ibid., 1.

27. Ibid.

28. Ibid., 6.

29. Alfred Philip Muntz, "Forests and Iron: The Charcoal Iron Industry of the New Jersey Highlands," *Geografiska Annaler, Advance and Retreat of Rural Settlement: Papers of the Siljan Symposium at the XIXth International Geographical Congress* 42, no. 4 (1960): 316.

30. Ibid., 318.

31. Ibid., 315.

32. Ibid., 316.

33. Ibid., 315.

34. Peter O. Wacker, *Land and People: A Cultural Geography of Preindustrial New Jersey: Origins and Settlement Patterns* (New Brunswick: Rutgers University Press, 1975), 3.

35. Ibid., 6.

36. Ibid.

37. Russell, "Vegetation of Northern New Jersey," 4. Occasionally, this lack of agricultural quality did not prevent some from trying to promote the area to potential settlers as an area for farming.

38. Muntz, "Forests and Iron," 315.

39. Ibid.

40. Ibid.

41. Merrill Jensen, "The American Revolution and American Agriculture," *Agricultural History* 43, no. 1 (January 1969), 108.

42. This is not to say of course that certain segments of the American colonial economy did not function adequately. "By 1776 there was a growing number of artisans who produced a wide variety of products for domestic consumption and for export to other colonies while ship building, iron production, and rum distilling approached the status of industries as the British [originally] conceived of them." From Jensen, "The American Revolution," 109.

43. Carl R. Woodward, "Agricultural Legislation in Colonial New Jersey," *Agricultural History* 3, no. 1 (January 1929), 16.

44. "The nature of crops produced and British legislation brought about distinct regional differences among the mainland Colonies and a distinct difference in their relationship with Britain." From Jensen, "The American Revolution," 110.

45. Woodward, "Agricultural Legislation," 17.

46. Jensen, "The American Revolution," 108. "Hence it was that American newspapers were filled with political news and crop and weather conditions even in such far-away places as Turkey and Russia, for what happened there might well affect the price of American wheat and corn"; Ibid., 109.

47. Ibid., 110.

48. Woodward, "Agricultural Legislation," 24.

49. In fact, merchants had a disproportionate amount of influence and power throughout the colonial and particularly during the early stages and through the Revolution. "The merchants of revolutionary America made up but a small part of the population, but they wielded economic and political power within most of the Colonies far out of proportion to their numbers." From Jensen, "The American Revolution," 109.

50. Woodward, "Agricultural Legislation," 18.

51. Ibid., 21.

52. As quoted in Jensen, "The American Revolution," 124.

53. Stephen Innes, ed., *Work and Labor in Early America* (Chapel Hill: University of North Carolina Press, 1988), 3.

IRON AND ECONOMICS

54. Harold C. Livesay, "Marketing Patterns in the Antebellum American Iron Industry," *Business History Review* 45, no. 3 (Autumn 1971), 270.

55. James M. Swank. *History of the Manufacture of Iron in All Ages and Particularly in the United States for Three Hundred Years, from 1585 to 1885* (Philadelphia: privately printed, 1884), 76.

56. Ibid.

57. John Smith, *Writings with Other Narratives of Roanoke, Jamestown, and the First English Settlement of America* (New York: The Library of America, 2007), 145.

58. These early exports were not all meant for England. Smith writes in the second book of his *The Generall Historie* that "Muscovia and Polonia doe yearely receive many thousands, for pitch, tarre, sope-ashes, Rosen, Flax, Cordage, Sturgeon, Masts, Yards, Wainscot, Firres, Glasse, and such like; also Swethland for Iron and Copper. France in like manner, for Wine, Canvas, and Salt. Spaine asmuch for Iron, Steele, Figges, Reasons, and Sackes." The initiative in Virginia certainly entertained an expansive proposal. This optimism was based on the seemingly unlimited resources that the early English settlers found in Virginia. Combine this with similar reports from northern explorations and it is no wonder England strove to "own" the North American colonies; Ibid., 281.

59. Ibid., 138.

60. Swank. *History of the Manufacture*, 112.

61. In book four of Captain John Smith's *The General History*, he lists a "Company of Ironmongers" in his list "The names of the Adventurers for Virginia…1620." This is very early, less than twenty years after Jamestown, for a cohesive group of industrialists organized for business in the iron industry. Smith, *Writings with Other Narratives*, 461.

62. Quoted in Swank, *History of the Manufacture*, 110.

63. Ibid.

64. Ibid.

65. Livesay, "Marketing Patterns," 270. The pig iron was shipped to England for processing and then exported back to America.

66. Swank, *History of the Manufacture*, 113.

67. Livesay, "Marketing Patterns," 272.

68. Robert B. Gordon, *American Iron, 1607–1900* (Baltimore: Johns Hopkins University Press, 1996), 1.

69. Livesay, "Marketing Patterns," 271.

70. Gordon, *American Iron*, 14.

71. Ibid., 15.

72. Livesay, "Marketing Patterns," 273.

73. The mines the Fords owned were of magnetite ore, which requited underground mining and left little surface evidence of such activities. The Mount Hope mine in Morris County began operation around 1710—the same year that John Ford began his forge in Hanover. From Gordon, *American Iron*, 30.

74. Ibid., 1.

75. Swank. *History of the Manufacture*, 114.
76. Ibid.
77. Ibid., 115.
78. Ibid. Blast meant that a furnace was capable of reaching the temperature necessary to produce the iron needed for ordnance were reached by introducing compressed hot air.
79. Ibid., 116.
80. Ibid., 117. As related by Swank from an address by Jacob W. Miller to the New Jersey Historical Society in 1854.
81. It should be pointed out that southern New Jersey had iron ore mines as well, although they were not as numerous or as well known.
82. Swank states that, "In 1784, New Jersey had eight furnaces and seventy-nine forges and bloomaries. In 1802 there were in New Jersey...150 forges, 'which, at a moderate calculation, would produce twenty tons of bar iron each annually, amounting to 3,000 tons.' At the same time there were in the state seven blast furnaces in operation." There were "about 120...in Morris, Sussex, and Bergen counties. Of the numerous charcoal furnaces which once dotted New Jersey not one now [1884] remains which uses charcoal, the introduction of anthracite coal in the smelting of iron ore, which took place about 1840, rendering the further production of charcoal pig iron in New Jersey unprofitable." From Swank. *History of the Manufacture*, 121.
83. Thayer, *Colonial and Revolutionary*, 55.
84. CLR, 14.
85. Thayer, *Colonial and Revolutionary*, 55.
86. Ibid., 65.
87. Ibid., 56.
88. Integrated Cultural Resource Report, Morristown National Historical Park. Draft, February 2001, 69. University of Massachusetts Archeological Services, Amherst, MA.
89. Ibid.
90. Ibid.
91. Ibid.
92. "The well-wooded hillsides and the restless mountain streams of Northern New Jersey afforded every facility for the manufacture of iron of a superior quality by this primitive [bloomer] method, while nearness of good markets furnished a sufficient inducement to engage in the business." From Swank, *History of the Manufacture*, 112.
93. Livesay, "Marketing Patterns," 274. "The first stage of iron manufacturing was smelting. This consisted of converting the ore into pig iron. At some furnaces iron was further refined and shaped into rough slabs called blooms. Pig iron was used by bloomeries (refiners) and foundries (processors); blooms went to forges and rolling mills. In either case the furnace owner faced

serious problems of distribution and finance. He usually had a large capital investment in ore pits, timber lands, furnaces, and horses and wagons to move the materials about. The remote location of many iron furnaces forced the owners to build living quarters for their employees"; Ibid.

94. Ibid.

95. Ibid., 275.

96. One issue was the chemical properties which the iron makers encountered. Trace amounts of certain chemicals would produce varying qualities of iron. "The presence of small amounts of elements…which only chemists could detect, caused large changes in the properties of iron and steel." From Gordon, *American Iron*, 20.

97. Fisher, *New Jersey as a Royal Province*, 273.

98. Laws were periodically passed in an attempt to conserve resources, though the motives were not totally preservation minded. Throughout the eighteenth century, laws regulating timber, oysters and cranberries were adopted in hopes of preventing a collapse of an industry through depletion of resources. From Woodward, "Agricultural Legislation," 23.

99. Integrated Cultural Resource Report, 27.

100. Muntz, "Forests and Iron," 322. As quoted by the author of the article.

101. Ibid.

102. Innes, ed., *Work and Labor*, 7.

103. Wacker, *Land and People*, xvi.

104. Ibid., xvii.

105. Swank. *History of the Manufacture*, 110.

106. John Ford does refer to himself as a carpenter in his will. This could have been the same type of pseudo-humility shown by Franklin D. Roosevelt when he referred to himself as a tree farmer on his tax return.

107. Arthur H. Cole, "The Tempo of Mercantile Life in Colonial America," *Business History Review* 33, no. 3 (Autumn 1959), 293.

108. Ibid.

109. "Small processing firms often operated quite successfully serving only a local market. As long as the proprietor was content to restrict the volume of production, he could buy his raw materials and sell his products without resorting to commercial intermediaries. Many firms did business exactly that way, remaining small through the proprietors lack of ambition, or because of inadequate transportation facilities to larger markets." From Livesay, "Marketing Patterns," 278.

110. Ibid., 273.

The Fords of New Jersey

111. In fact, the policy of quitrent payments was "a survival of late feudal times when a money payment came to be accepted in lieu of food and labor owed

to the lord of the manor." Or, in this case, to the proprietors. From Wacker, *Land and People*, 224.

112. Fisher, *New Jersey as a Royal Province*, 176.

113. CLR, 13.

114. Eleanor M. Bamford. "Ford Family Notes," *New York Genealogical and Biographical Record* 53 (1922), 160–175.

115. Ibid., 165. Jacob Ford Sr. seems to have used the second "f" more often, although his father did as well. The last known usage of it is in Ford Sr.'s 1777 will.

116. While the Fords were very wealthy, they were not of the colonial gentry who ruled or governed colonies. Their influence was more localized and tended not to venture beyond their business interests.

117. Bamford. "Ford Family Notes," 165.

118. Frances Bazley Lee. *Genealogical and Memorial History of the State of New Jersey Volume IV.* (New York: Lewis Historical Publishing Company, 1910), 1,563.

119. Ibid.

120. Although depending on how this is calculated, that amount could at the high end be worth as much as £1,000,000 today. Although a more sober estimate would be around £500,000–700,000, still a considerable amount of money. Lawrence H. Officer, "Purchasing Power of British Pounds from 1264 to Present," MeasuringWorth, 2009. http://www.measuringworth. com/ppoweruk/ (accessed March 1, 2010).

121. Discussion and quotations in this section come from the Last Will and Testament of Hannah Ford at the New Jersey State Archives.

122. Discussion and quotations in this section come from the Last Will and Testament of Jacob Ford Jr. at the New Jersey State Archives.

123. Lee. *Genealogical and Memorial History*, 1,564.

124. Ibid., 1,565.

125. Discussion and quotations in this section come from the Last Will and Testament of Theodosia Ford at the New Jersey State Archives.

126. Discussion and quotations in this section come from manuscripts in the Ford Family Papers, Morristown (New Jersey) National Historical Park, box 6, folders 4:30–4:32.

127. This figure equates roughly to between one-quarter and half a million dollars in 2010. Lawrence H. Officer, "Six Ways to Compute the Relative Value of a U.S. Dollar Amount, 1774 to Present." MeasuringWorth, 2009. http://www.measuringworth.com/uscompare/ (accessed March 1, 2010).

128. The two letters that most accurately describe the issues involved in the settling of the estate of Theodosia Ford are two that Henry Ford wrote to those in line to inherit. In particular, those which he addressed to his uncle judge Henry De Saussure (second director of the United States mint) in South Carolina. The two are provided (with modern grammar, etc.) in full:

January 27, 1825. Dear Uncle, The foregoing copy of the last will and testament of my deceased grandmother, and of the inventory and appraisement of the personal estate, are truly made from the originals. The goods and furniture appraised at $154.12 in the inventory. My father offered to take altogether at $120. They might not bring this amount at a cash sale, but they might at the usual credit of six months. The [?] and dispersion of money in small sums about the country occasions however a troublesome collection, and in defiance of every precaution will generate some hazard of loss. I shall wait for the opinion of legatees before I adopt either mode of disposition. I think the money may be collected on the bonds by the beginning of July. The contracts which are well secured, carry an interest of seven per cent, and since the reduction of the rate of interest to six in this state on new contracts, a benefit of one per cent might induce some purchasers to cash them, if the obligors failed to be punctual at the time I have appointed. I will advise you further as soon as I am able. To the memory of my grandmother I propose to rest a slab of brown horizontal stone similar to those over most of our ancestors. As the little brick walls that are moldering that support two of those, my father proposes they be repaired at the same time. The expense will be but trifling. Please do give me your advice on these subjects. Henry Ford.

April 28, 1827, Dear Uncle, The delay in settling the estate of my grandmother has been far greater than was expected and which was also unavoidable unless ruinous measures had been used to coerce payment of the debt. By a prosecution against Moses Phillips the sheriff has a [?] upon all his property in this county and he was continually sending me imploring [?] letters from the state of New York not to ruin him by a sale, proposing from time to time unavailing modes of satisfaction. At length I assigned the [?] to Robert Thomson of the city of New York, receiving from him $3,137.72 the principal of the bond. As to the interest I took safe notes to the amount, endorsed and payable and at [?]. George Strehle[?] an industrious man and always prompt in payment of interest to my grandmother had his forge available stock of coal on another property destroyed by fire about the same time that his bond and mortgage were called. To have insisted upon immediate payment would have broken him up [?] required all his active means to reinstate [?] a day or two ago. I induced Mr. Macculloch to take assignment [?] of the mortgage and he paid me the amount due on the bond. The sheriff has advertised Miller's property for sale [?] and about the time the above note will be due and expect to receive this debt. [?] perceive by a concise statement amended that there is a balance in my hands for [?] of fifteen hundred 33/100 dollars at this time. How shall I dispose of it? I can deposit it in the branch bank of the United States or in any other bank in the city of New York to your credit subject to your draft or I will remit it in any other way you may desire. I shall endeavor to close the affairs of this estate at the next July term of the orphan's court of this county I trust without any material loss *to the legatees. The turnpike stock however is poor. The most that has been offered for it is $8 per share which cost originally about $20. Henry Ford.*

129. Judith M. Jacob, "Historic Structure Report Ford Mansion," Morristown National Historical Park, NPS, Draft, October 1993, 4.

130. In addition to his business interests, Gabriel Ford was as noted a well-regarded jurist. As was typical of the time, he had a lucrative part-time job in training young men for the law. Before law schools, students read law with an established lawyer and worked almost as a paralegal of today would do to learn the vocation. One such young man who read with Gabriel Ford was Isaac Blackford. Blackford was born and raised in New Jersey but eventually moved to Indiana. There he became the celebrated jurist known as "The Indiana Blackstone." Blackford studied with Judge Ford between the years 1808–1810. Later in his life he wrote of the excellent training he received from Judge Ford and of the thrill of getting to spend a night in the Washington bedroom at the Ford Mansion. Blackford told of the room and the original furnishings still there from Washington's time. From W.W. Thornton, *Isaac Blackford, The Indiana Blackstone.* (Indianapolis: Indiana Supreme Court, n.d.), 5.

131. Discussion and quotations in this section come from manuscripts in the Ford Family Papers, Morristown NHP, box 9, folders 6:5–6:15; box 10, folder 6:25.

132. Discussion and quotations in this section come from the Last Will and Testament of Gabriel Ford at the New Jersey State Archives.

133. Monore was a small village just east of present day Morristown. It was settled in 1715 by John Ford and at the time was known as Fordville. By the mid-nineteenth century, a larger village named after President Monroe enveloped Fordville before itself being absorbed into the greater Morristown, Hanover, Whippany area.

134. For a more in depth discussion on the disposition of the mansion, see Pfister, *The Jacob Ford Jr. Mansion.*

135. Discussion and quotations in this section come from the inventory of Henry A. Ford, November 1872 at the New Jersey State Archives.

136. See Pfister, *The Jacob Ford Jr. Mansion,* for a detailed account of the sale of the mansion and the surrounding controversy.

137. See Pfister, *The Jacob Ford Jr. Mansion,* for a fuller account of the transformation of the mansion from family home to a national historical park.

BUSINESS DETAILS

138. Discussion and quotations in this section come from manuscripts in the Ford Family Papers, Morristown NHP, box 15, folders 10:1–10:18.

139. Ibid.

140. Ibid.
141. Proclamation money was money as proclaimed by Queen Anne in 1704 in an effort to standardize currency in the American colonies and within the empire.

Mrs. Ford and John Jacob Faesch

142. Discussion and quotations in this section come from manuscripts in the Ford Family Papers, Morristown NHP, box 15, folders 10:1–10:18.

A Difference of Opinion

143. Discussion and quotations in this section come from manuscripts in the Ford Family Papers, Morristown NHP, box 15, folders 10:1–10:18.
144. Timothy Ford's report is not known to exist.

Canfield et al. v. Faesch et al.

145. Discussion and quotations in this section come from manuscripts in the Ford Family Papers, Morristown NHP, box 2, folders 1:30–1:40. The defendants' answer to the complaint against the Faesch estate will be utilized almost exclusively as it is the most detailed.

Ford v. Tuttle

146. Discussion and quotations in this section come from manuscripts in the Ford Family Papers, Morristown NHP, box 2, folders 2:6–2:13; box 3, folders 2:14–2:15.

The Geology of New Jersey

147. This appendix is from the New Jersey Department of Environmental Protection at http://www.state.nj.us/dep/njgs/ (accessed August 3, 2010).

BIBLIOGRAPHY

This work is nearly entirely fashioned out of the resources contained in the Ford Family Papers; part of the Morristown National Historical Park archival collection. Of necessity, an entire second collection was avoided to keep this work within a reasonable length. It is strongly encouraged that anyone with more interest in researching this story should contact the Morristown NHP archives for information on how to access the collection for research. Information on researching at the park library can be found at: http://www. morristownnhplibrary.blogspot.com/.

There are many fine studies of New Jersey available today. Both in print and out-of-print works offer a variety of general and scholarly approaches to the various periods and events in the state's long and sometimes colorful history. While this book claims no particular originality in terms of the overall presentation of the state's history, it does claim a unique approach to the layering of family and state history in a meaningful way for the benefit of the reader. Furthermore, it is hoped that reexamining some basic points in New Jersey's history will encourage a new audience to explore more of the state's heritage.

It has been referred to that the Ford Family Papers at the Morristown NHP archives are a virtually unknown and hence underutilized resource. The same could be said for the even more unknown Cobb papers at the Morristown NHP archives. While this work relied heavily on the Ford papers, much was left out by necessity. Therefore, plenty of material exists for further study. The Cobb papers, as a wholly untapped resource, represent a new venue for someone looking for an original topic.

The books listed here are simply those consulted in the writing of and preparation of the current work. It is advised that the bibliographies of the works listed be consulted further for even more information concerning New Jersey.

WILLS AND DEEDS/BONDS

Generally, in discussion of the wills, and in the quotations of wills, the eighteenth century language and punctuation has been modernized to facilitate reading. Footnotes are not provided for sections of the wills of the family member quoted. Anyone wishing to study or research the originals in their sometimes arcane language is encouraged to make an appointment with the New Jersey state archives staff. All originals are maintained at the state archives and can be easily referenced there. Morristown NHP also holds copies of the originals for research.

SECONDARY SOURCES/BOOKS

Bamford, Eleanor M. "Ford Family Notes." Pages 160–170 in *The New York Genealogical and Biographical Record*. New York: New York Genealogical and Biographical Society, 1922.

Fisher, Edgar Jacob. *New Jersey as a Royal Province 1738 to 1776*. New York: Columbia University, 1911.

Gordon, Robert B. *American Iron, 1607–1900*. Baltimore: Johns Hopkins University Press, 1960.

Hamilton, Phillip. *The Making and Unmaking of a Revolutionary Family; The Tuckers of Virginia, 1752–1830*. Charlottesville: The University of Virginia Press, 2003.

Innes, Stephen, ed. *Work and Labor in Early America*. Chapel Hill: University of North Carolina Press, 1988.

Lee, Frances Bazley. *Genealogical and Memorial History of the State of New Jersey Volume IV*. New York: Lewis Historical Publishing Company, 1910.

Pomfret, John E. *The Province of East New Jersey 1609–1702: The Rebellious Proprietary*. Princeton: Princeton University Press, 1962.

Smith, John. *Writings with Other Narratives of Roanoke, Jamestown, and the First English Settlement of America*. New York: Library of America, 2007.

Swank, James M. *History of the Manufacture of Iron in All Ages and Particularly in the United States for Three Hundred Years, from 1585 to 1885*. Philadelphia: privately printed, 1884.

Thayer, Theodore. *Colonial and Revolutionary Morris County*. Morristown, NJ: Morris County Heritage Commission, 1975.

Wacker, Peter O. *Land and People, A Cultural Geography of Preindustrial New Jersey: Origins and Settlement Patterns*. New Brunswick: Rutgers University Press, 1975.

ARTICLES

Jensen, Merrill. "The American Revolution and American Agriculture." *Agricultural History* 43, no. 1 (January 1969), 107–124.

Livesay, Harold C. "Marketing Patterns in the Antebellum American Iron Industry." *Business History Review* 45, no. 3 (Autumn 1971), 269–295.

Muntz, Alfred Philip. "Forests and Iron: The Charcoal Iron Industry of the New Jersey Highlands." *Geografiska Annaler, Advance and Retreat of Rural Settlement: Papers of the Siljan Symposium at the XIXth International Geographical Congress* 42, no. 4 (1960), 315–323.

Russell, Emily W. B. "Vegetation of Northern New Jersey Before European Settlement." *American Midland Naturalist* 105, no. 1 (January 1981), 1–12.

Woodward, Carl R. "Agricultural Legislation in Colonial New Jersey." *Agricultural History* 3, no. 1 (January 1929), 15–28.

NATIONAL PARK SERVICE REPORTS

Craig, Vera B., and Ralph H. Lewis. "Furnishings Plan for the Ford Mansion (1779–1780)," Morristown National Historical Park, 1976.

"Integrated Cultural Resource Report, Morristown National Historical Park." Draft, University of Massachusetts Archeological Services, Amherst, MA, February 2001.

Massey, William U. "Historical Grounds survey of Washington's Headquarters the Ford Mansion." Morristown: May 1975.

"Morristown National Historical Park Cultural Landscape Report for Washington's Headquarters." National Park Service, Olmsted Center for Landscape Preservation, Boston, 2005.

WEBSITES

New Jersey Department of Environmental Protection, http://www.state.nj.us/dep/njgs/ (accessed August 5, 2010).

Officer, Lawrence H. "Purchasing Power of British Pounds from 1264 to Present," MeasuringWorth, 2009. http://www.measuringworth.com/ppoweruk/ (accessed March 1, 2010).

———. "Six Ways to Compute the Relative Value of a U.S. Dollar Amount, 1774 to Present." MeasuringWorth, 2009. http://www.measuringworth.com/uscompare/ (accessed March 1, 2010).

Index

ABOUT THE AUTHOR

D r. Jude Pfister has been at Morristown since 2004 and has been with the National Park Service in the field of historic preservation and cultural resource conservation since 1993. Prior to 1993, he worked for the Delaware State Archives. Dr. Pfister oversees the museum, archival and library programs at Morristown and has as his goal the integration of the separate disciplines into a single unit representing our cultural heritage. He has experience in a variety of curatorial settings impacting many of our nation's most important historic sites and collections. His professional interests include American constitutional development; the development of American historiography as a separate discipline; historic preservation and the communication of cultural patrimony to the general public; and understanding the broad scope of historic preservation through the interconnectedness of cultural resources. He earned his bachelor of arts degree from Delaware State University in 1991, his master's degree from Washington College in 1993 and his doctorate from Drew University in

Photo by Sarah Minegar.

2007. He is the author of *The First Decade of the United States Supreme Court*, *The Jacob Ford Jr. Mansion* and several articles and reviews. In 2010, his book *The Jacob Ford Jr. Mansion* was awarded the Eastern National Board of Directors Author's Award. He also lectures regularly.